INTRODUCING
Word *for* Windows

Carol McKenzie • Pat Bryden

Heinemann Educational
a division of Heinemann Publishers (Oxford) Ltd,
Halley Court, Jordan Hill, Oxford OX2 8EJ

OXFORD LONDON EDINBURGH MADRID ATHENS BOLOGNA
PARIS MELBOURNE SYDNEY AUCKLAND SINGAPORE TOKYO
IBADAN NAIROBI HARARE GABORONE PORTSMOUTH NH (USA)

© Carol McKenzie and Patricia Bryden 1995

First Published 1995

95 96 97 98 11 10 9 8 7 6 5 4 3 2 1

A catalogue record for this book is available from the British Library on request.

ISBN 0 435 454188

Designed by Raynor Design using QuarkXPress 3.3™ on the Apple Macintosh™

Printed in Great Britain by Thomson Litho Ltd, East Kilbride, Scotland

Screen shots reprinted with permission from Microsoft Corporation

Contents

About this book		1
Introduction to Word for Windows		3
Unit 1	**Key in and edit text, save and print a file**	7
	Open a new document	
	Key in text	
	Delete/insert text	
	Move around the text: quick methods	
	Save and name a document	
	Splitting paragraphs, joining paragraphs	
	Save a document (previously named)	
	Scrolling the text (using the mouse)	
	Print a document	
	Close a file	
	Exit from Word for Windows	
Unit 2	**Select text, move and copy text**	17
	Open an existing file	
	Selecting text	
	Delete a block of text	
	Quick delete and insert text	
	Restore deleted text (undo)	
	Move a block of text	
	Copy a block of text	
Unit 3	**Change format, margins and line spacing, print preview**	22
	Formatting the right margin	
	Ragged (unjustified) right margin	
	Justified right margin	
	Changing left and right margins	
	Change the units of measurement	
	Margins	
	Line spacing – single and double	
	Print preview	
	Editing in print preview	
	Printing from print preview	
Unit 4	**Find (search) and replace text, spelling tool**	29
	Find (search) and replace	
	Find text	
	Spelling check	
	Spelling tool	
Unit 5	**Formatting/emphasizing text**	34
	Bold, underline, italics, font typeface, font size, centred text	
Unit 6	**Consolidation 1**	38

Unit 7	**Examination practice 1**	**41**
Unit 8	**Unfamiliar and foreign words**	**43**
Unit 9	**Text editing, grammar tool**	**45**
	Typescript containing correction signs	
	Typescript containing abbreviations	
	Typescript containing typographical errors	
	Typescript containing errors of agreement	
	Grammar tool	
Unit 10	**Working from manuscript copy**	**51**
	Typing from manuscript copy	
	Additional correction signs	
Unit 11	**Personal business letters**	**54**
	Keying in a personal business letter	
	Envelopes	
	Insert a new page break	
Unit 12	**Consolidation 2**	**59**
Unit 13	**Examination practice 2**	**61**
Unit 14	**Tabulation**	**63**
	Set tabs, delete tabs, move tabs, change tab alignment, default tabs	
Unit 15	**Memorandums and abbreviations**	**67**
	Memorandum	
	Abbreviations	
Unit 16	**Indent text, change line length, enumerated paragraphs**	**69**
	Indent – 'wrap around' or temporary indent feature	
	To indent a paragraph	
	Changing the typing line length	
	Enumerated or bulleted paragraphs	
Unit 17	**Allocating vertical space and confirming facts**	**75**
	Allocating vertical space (using paragraph format command)	
	Confirming facts	
Unit 18	**Business letter layout**	**79**
	Business letter layout	
	Special marks and enclosure marks	
	Automatic date insertion	
Unit 19	**Rearranging text**	**85**
Unit 20	**Consolidation 3**	**90**
Unit 21	**Examination practice 3**	**93**
Print-out checks		**97**
Progress review checklist		**118**
Glossary		**119**

About this book

The first part of the book is an introduction to the Windows environment and the techniques needed for the use of the Word for Windows software package. It is anticipated that users will be familiar with the QWERTY keyboard and have basic competence in using computer hardware. Students will learn how to communicate through the graphical user interface, using both the mouse and keyboard.

Units 1 – 7 are designed for students preparing to take basic examinations such as RSA CLAIT (word-processing application). These units are also suitable for beginners who wish to learn basic text-processing skills without taking an examination.

Units 8 – 13 are designed for students preparing to take basic examinations such as RSA Core Text Processing Skills. These units are also suitable for beginners who wish to learn basic text-editing skills and the preparation of a personal business letter without taking an examination.

Units 14 – 21 are designed for students preparing to take elementary examinations such as RSA Stage I Text/Word Processing, Pitman Elementary, City & Guilds Level I and NVQ Level 1 units in administration. These units are also suitable for students who wish to extend their knowledge and skills to include simple tabulation, text formatting, preparation of memorandums, and business letters without taking an examination.

Format of the book

Consolidation practice for each stage of learning is included in Units 6, 12 and 20. **Examination practice** for each stage of learning is included in Units 7, 13 and 21, covering the requirements of examinations offered by RSA, Pitman Examinations Institute and City & Guilds.

Print-out checks for all exercises are given at the back of the book. These should be used for checking by both students and teachers/trainers. The **progress review checklist** allows students to keep a record of progress through the exercises, noting the number of errors made. If completed at the end of each working session, the student can refer to this checklist to locate without delay the unit to be worked next.

Command boxes for Word for Windows functions are given when appropriate. Instruction is given on how to carry out the required function. The commands explain keyboard, mouse and menu operation.

The glossary provides a comprehensive, alphabetically listed quick reference for all the Word for Windows commands introduced in the book. The commands are shown for keyboard, mouse and menu users. **Shortcut keys** are included and students may prefer to use these methods as they become more familiar with the program.

Working through a unit

1. When you see this symbol, read all the information before you begin. You may also need to refer back to this information as you carry out the exercises.

2. When you see this symbol, carry out the exercises, following the numbered steps, e.g. 1.1, 1.2.

3. Use your spelling tool to check your document. Proof-read your document carefully – the spelling tool does not find every error.

4. Use the Print Preview facility to check that your document is going to be correct when printed. If it is, save your work on to your floppy disk (usually in A drive). Then print your work.

5. Compare your document with the print-out checks at the back of the book. (If you are using this book in class, your tutor may also wish to check your work.) Correct any errors which you find in your work. Print the documents again if required to do so by your tutor. (If you are working on your own, you may not consider this necessary.)

6. Complete your progress review checklist. Then exit from Word for Windows or begin work on the next unit (as appropriate).

Do not delete files from your disk – you will need them later!

Introduction to Word for Windows

Microsoft Windows is a graphical user interface which allows the user to communicate with the computer. The graphical nature of the messages on screen makes Windows a user-friendly operating system. **Word for Windows** is a software package used for text processing which operates within the Windows environment.

When you start the Word for Windows program, the following **document window** will be displayed on screen:

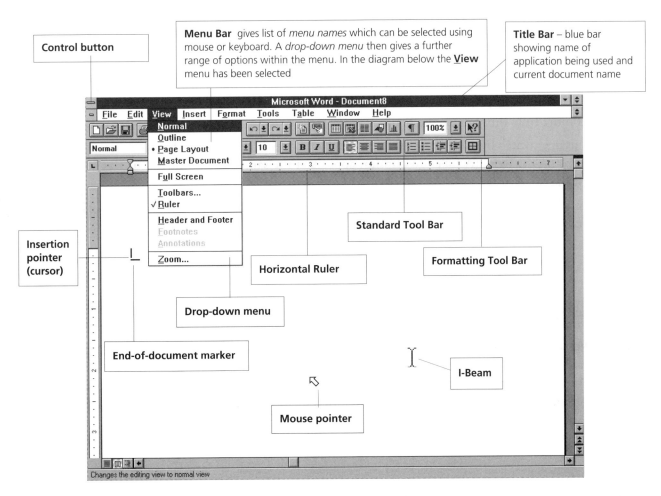

When Word is carrying out a function, it may ask you to wait. The icon for this is the **hourglass** ⧖. Wait until the hourglass has disappeared from the screen before proceeding with the next step.

The **status bar** at the bottom of the screen displays information about the document on screen, e.g. the page number, section number, line number, column number, etc. For example:

| Page 3 | Sec 1 | 3/3 | At 1" | Ln 1 | Col 10 | 10:21 |

Menu

To select an option from the menu you can either:

- use the keyboard – press the underlined letter for the required menu option
- use the mouse – click the mouse pointer on the option required
- use a keyboard shortcut, e.g. **Ctrl + F** selects the **F**ind menu option (holding down the **Ctrl** key and then pressing the letter shown will activate the command)

A **tick** against a menu choice indicates that the option is currently in operation. When the tick is removed, the facility is 'switched off'. An **ellipsis** after a menu choice (e.g. **Z**oom ...) indicates that you will be asked to give more information before the command can be executed.

Toolbars

To select an icon from the Standard or Formatting Tool Bar you:

- Click the mouse pointer on the icon.

Each icon on the toolbars represents a different function. For example, clicking on the print icon would activate the printer to print a copy of the current document. The use of icons is explained more fully throughout the book.

The function activated by each icon is shown in a **Tool Tip** which appears when the mouse pointer is positioned on the icon. (A fuller description appears at the same time in the **Status Bar** at the bottom of the screen.)

When you click on an icon button it is 'highlighted' to show that the function is currently in operation.

The **Bold** Tool Tip

Dialogue box

When Word needs to give or receive more information, a **dialogue box** is displayed on screen. You can move through the dialogue box using the **Tab key** or the **Arrow** keys on the keyboard, or you can use the mouse to move to the section you need. Word for Windows asks you to respond by presenting information, options or questions in different ways by using boxes and buttons (see below).

INTRODUCTION TO WORD FOR WINDOWS

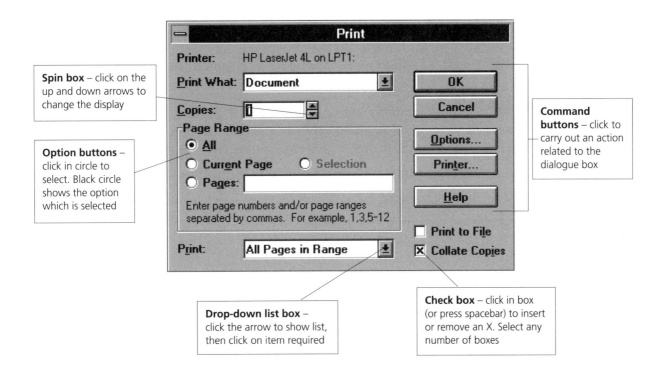

The Scroll Bars

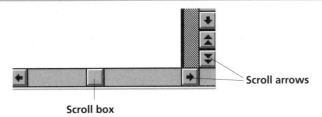

The **Scroll Bars** at the right side and bottom of the screen allow text to be scrolled by the use of the mouse, e.g. clicking on the ▼ button will move the 'document frame' downwards so that the text moves up the screen. Scrolling is more fully explained in Unit 1.

The Scroll Bar also displays buttons to select the different ways in which a document can be viewed. These are more fully explained in Unit 3.

Using the mouse

The mouse is used to move a pointer to any required location on screen. The mouse has two buttons: **left** and **right**. As you move the mouse across the desk, an electronic sensor picks up the movement of the ball and moves the **mouse pointer** across the screen in the same direction.

- You use the mouse to *point* to the item you want on screen.
- You then *click* the mouse button (usually the left one) to highlight or *select* an option on screen (quickly pressing and releasing the button).
- Sometimes you *double-click* a mouse button (quickly pressing and releasing the button twice).
- You may also use a *dragging* action by holding down the mouse button, moving the mouse and then releasing the button.

The Help Menu

Word for Windows offers on-line **Help** to users. The help command can be activated in two ways from the document screen:

- By selecting **H**elp from the Menu Bar
- By clicking on the [?] icon on the Standard Tool Bar and then clicking on the feature on screen or keying in the name of the feature with which you require help

Selecting **C**ontents from the Help drop-down menu gives a list of the features available, e.g.

Examples and Demos
Visual examples and demonstrations to help you learn Word

Using Word
Step-by-step instructions to help you complete your tasks

Selecting **S**earch for Help on ... from the Help drop-down menu gives you the opportunity to key in the name of the feature with which you require help.

Selecting **I**ndex displays an alphabetical list of functions and features. You can move quickly through the list by clicking on the alphabetical button of the feature you require at the top of the Index screen.

Selecting **Quick Preview** activates a learning program which introduces you to Word for Windows.

Selecting **E**xamples and Demos allows you to access demonstrations of a range of Word features.

UNIT 1
Key in and edit text, save and print a file

At the end of Unit 1 you will have learnt how to
- *load Word for Windows*
- *open a new file*
- *key in text*
- *move around the text using the mouse, the arrow keys and the scroll bar*
- *edit text – delete/insert characters or words*
- *split and join paragraphs*
- *proof-read your work carefully*
- *save your document to your personal disk*
- *print your file*
- *clear the screen by closing a file*
- *exit from Word for Windows*

Follow the instructions step by step

1.1 Load Windows and select Word for Windows by double-clicking on the icon *Microsoft Word*

The application window (Microsoft Word) will be displayed on screen. Refer to the Introduction to refresh your memory on this.

1.2 Open a new document using one of the following methods.

Open a new document

Keyboard	Mouse
Press: **Ctrl** + N	Select: **File** from the Menu Bar
	Select: **New** from the **File** drop-down menu
	or
	Click: **New (New file)** button on the Standard Tool Bar

The **New** dialogue box is displayed on screen:

Check that your dialogue box matches the one shown above.

- **Normal** in the **Template** box means that Word will use standard preset margins and fonts.
- **Document** means that your work will be saved in document format.
- Position the mouse pointer over the **OK** button and click the left mouse button.

Key in text

Wordwrap	When you key in text, you do not need to press ↵ (return/enter) at the end of each line as Word for Windows will automatically do this for you.
Initial capitals	To type an initial capital (first letter of word): Press: **Shift** key + **letter**
Closed capitals	(All letters in capitals): Press: **Caps Lock** key (to start typing in capitals) Press: **Caps Lock** again to stop
Clear lines Press: ↵ twice	To leave a blank line, e.g. between paragraphs: *Note:* You should leave at least one clear line after headings. You should leave one clear line space between paragraphs and different parts of a document.
Punctuation	
Full stop	No space before; one or two spaces after – be consistent.

Comma	No space before, one space after.
Question/exclamation mark	Same as full stop because they are used at end of sentence.
Colon(:) Two spaces after when followed by a capital letter One space after when followed by a lower-case letter.	No space before
Semi-colon(;)	No space before, one space after.
Brackets and single/double quotation marks No spaces immediately inside the signs.	One space before the opening sign One space after the closing sign

Exercise 1A

1.3 Refer to the information section above, 'Key in text'. Key in the following text – do not worry if you make mistakes; you can correct them later.

> When you start using Word for Windows, your screen will show the name of the application in the bar at the top. Immediately below this you will see the menu bar, containing a horizontal list of words, each with the initial letter underlined. You can select an item in the menu bar by using the mouse or the keyboard: If you wish to use the mouse, you should move the mouse pointer to the required item and then 'click' the mouse button. If you wish to use the keyboard, you should hold down the Alt key and then press the keyboard key corresponding to the underlined letter.

1.4 As you keyed in the above text, you should have noticed a vertical black line **l** at the point where you were inserting text. This is the insertion pointer and it moves along as you key in text. The arrow keys (← ↑ → ↓) to the right of the main keyboard allow you to move the insertion pointer around the text one space or one line at a time.

Practise moving the insertion pointer around the text you have just keyed in using the arrow keys.

1.5 The insertion pointer can also be moved around the text by using the mouse. If you move the mouse on your desk, you will see the *I*-beam moving correspondingly on screen. If the left-hand mouse button is clicked, the *I*-beam changes into the insertion pointer.

Practise positioning the insertion pointer in the text you have just keyed in, using the mouse and the *I*-beam.

1.6 Check the text you have keyed in very carefully. If you find any errors, correct them now by positioning the insertion pointer at the appropriate place and deleting or inserting characters or words as required, using the commands shown below.

Delete/insert text

Keyboard/mouse

To delete (erase) an incorrect character:

Position **insertion pointer** immediately *after* character to be deleted
Press: ← **Del** (the backspace delete key)
or
Position **insertion pointer** immediately *before* character to be deleted
Press: **Del**(ete)

To insert a character (or characters):

Position **insertion pointer** where the text is to be inserted. Key in the text (the existing text will move across to make space for the new text)

1.7 Position the pointer after the full stop at the end of the text on screen. Press ↵ twice to start a new paragraph. Key in the following text under your previous work:

> The choice of keyboard or mouse operation is a personal one. It is generally considered that the keyboard system is faster as the operator's fingers are usually hovering over the 'QWERTY' section. However, you may prefer to use the mouse at first until you have learned all the keyboard commands. You may also find it quicker to move the insertion pointer when editing by using the mouse.
>
> Be aware of both systems and practise them while you are learning to use the program.
>
> When you have become proficient through regular practice, you may find that you have adopted a combination of mouse and keyboard use, automatically selecting the quickest or most suitable system for the task in hand.

1.8 You have already practised moving around the text using the arrow keys and the mouse pointer. In Word for Windows you can move around the text more quickly using the keyboard keys. If you learn and practise these commands, you will become more proficient. Some of these commands are particularly useful in a long document.

Practise moving the insertion pointer around the text you have just keyed in using the following keyboard commands.

Moving around the text: quick methods

To move	Keyboard
Left word by word	Press: **Ctrl+** ← (arrow key) (hold down the Ctrl key and press the ← key while the **Ctrl** key is still held down)
Right word by word	Press: **Ctrl + →**
To the end of the line	Press: **End**
To the start of the line	Press: **Home**
To top of paragraph	Press: **Ctrl + ↑**
To bottom of paragraph	Press: **Ctrl + ↓**
Up one screen	Press: **Page Up**
Down one screen	Press: **Page Down**
To the top of the document	Press: **Ctrl + Home**
To the bottom of the document	Press: **Ctrl + End**

1.9 Check the text you have keyed in very carefully, comparing it with the exercises. If you find any errors, correct them now by moving the insertion pointer to the appropriate position and delete or insert characters or words as required.

1.10 Follow the instructions 'Save and name a document' to save your document on Drive A using filename **EX1A**.

 Save and name a document

Keyboard	Mouse
Press: **Ctrl** + **S** *or* **F12** (function key at top of keyboard)	Select: **F**ile from the Menu Bar Select: **Save As ...** from the **F**ile drop-down menu

The **Save As** dialogue box is displayed on screen:

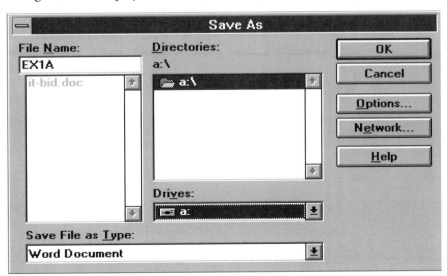

Select from the **Save As** dialogue buttons as follows:

- Click on **File Name** box and key in **EX1A**
- Click on ↓ at side of **Drives** box and select **a:**
- Check that **Save File as Type** box shows **Word Document**
- Check that **Directories** box shows **a:**
- Click on **OK** box

Note: You can move between the different sections of a dialogue box by using the tab key or by positioning and clicking the left mouse button.

'Word is saving EX1A.DOC' should appear in the status line at the bottom of the screen.

Wait until the hourglass icon has disappeared from screen – long documents can take some time to save. The document should remain on your screen.

1.11 The first draft of a document is often edited. The writer may decide to delete or insert words or to make other changes. You have already learnt how to delete and insert text.

 Splitting paragraphs, joining paragraphs

As part of editing a document, it may be necessary to split a block of text into two or more smaller paragraphs. It may also be necessary to join two or more paragraphs to make a larger paragraph.

To split a block of text into two paragraphs:

- Position insertion pointer immediately before first letter of intended second paragraph
- Press: ↵ twice

To join two paragraphs into one:

- Position insertion pointer immediately before first letter of second paragraph
- Press: **Del** (delete backspace) twice

Exercise 1A continued

Practise editing the text you saved as EX1A by referring to the instructions given. Make the following changes to the document on screen as shown below:

- delete any words crossed out
- insert text at points marked ⋀
- make new paragraphs at all the points marked // or [
- join the paragraphs at the run on sign (⌒)
- in the last two paragraphs, change the word **system** to **method**

When you start using Word for Windows, your screen will show the name of the application in the **title** bar at the top. Immediately below this you will see the menu bar, containing a horizontal list of words, each with the initial letter underlined. You can select an item in the menu bar by using the mouse or the keyboard: If you wish to use the mouse, you should move the mouse pointer to the required item and then 'click' the **left** mouse button. If you wish to use the keyboard, you should hold down the Alt key and then press the keyboard key corresponding to the **initial** underlined letter.

The choice of keyboard or mouse operation is a personal one. It is generally considered that the keyboard system is faster as the operator's fingers are usually hovering over the 'QWERTY' section. However, you may prefer to use the mouse at first until you have learned all the keyboard commands. You may also find it quicker to move the insertion pointer when editing by using the mouse.

Be aware of both **techniques** and practise them while you are learning to use the program.

When you have become proficient through regular practice, you may find that you have adopted a combination of mouse and keyboard use, automatically selecting the quickest or most suitable system for the task in hand.

1.12 Check your work on screen, comparing it with the exercise. When you are satisfied that your document is completely accurate, follow the instructions under 'Save a document (previously named)' to save the changes you have made.

Save a document (previously named)

You should use this method when you want to save a document under the same name when you have amended it.

The document on screen was saved under filename EX1A before you carried out the changes. The amended document can now be resaved using the same filename.

Keyboard	Mouse
Press: **Ctrl + S**	Select: **F**ile from the Menu Bar
or	Select: **S**ave from the **F**ile drop-down menu
Press: **Shift +** F12	*or*
	Click: **Save** button on the Standard Toolbar

'Word is fast saving EX1A.DOC' should appear in the status line at the bottom of the screen.

Wait until the hourglass icon has disappeared from screen – long documents can take some time to save. The document should remain on your screen.

1.13 You have already practised moving around the text using the arrow keys, the mouse pointer and the keyboard quick methods. In Word for Windows, the text can be moved up and down the screen (scrolling). In scrolling, the insertion pointer stays in the same position but the text moves up or down.

Refer to the Introduction to refresh your memory on scroll bars and scroll buttons.

14 KEY IN AND EDIT TEXT, SAVE AND PRINT A FILE

 Scrolling the text (using the mouse)

To scroll the text	Mouse
One line at a time	Click: Up and down scroll arrows
One screen at a time	Click: In the grey scroll bar immediately underneath or above the appropriate scroll arrow
Quickly over larger distances	Click and drag: The thumb box on the scroll bar (the bottom left of the status line tells you where you are within the document)
or	
Click anywhere in the scroll bar	

 1.14 Your first document (EX1A) should now be amended and saved. To print a copy of the document, follow the instructions under 'Print a document'.

 Print a document

Keyboard	Mouse
Press: **Ctrl + P**	Select: **File** from the Menu Bar Select: **Print** from the **File** drop-down menu *or* Click: **Print** button on the Standard Toolbar

The **Print** dialogue box is displayed on screen:

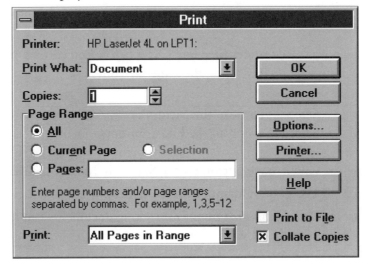

Printer: The name of the printer should be displayed

Print What: Allows choice of what is to be printed – normally displays **Document**

Copies: Allows choice of number of copies printed – normally displays **1**

Page Range: Allows selection of pages printed – normally displays **All**

Print: Allows certain pages to be printed – normally displays **All Pages in Range**

Click on **OK**

'**Word is preparing to background print EX1A.DOC**' should appear in the status line at the bottom of the screen.

Wait until the hourglass icon has disappeared from screen – long documents can take some time to print. The document remains on your screen.

1.15 Check your print-out with that at the back of the book. If you find any errors, correct them on screen, save your document again and print again if necessary.

1.16 Follow the instructions under 'Close a file'.

Close a file

After saving and printing in Word for Windows, the document remains on screen. Close the file before opening another one, or before exiting the program.

Mouse/menu

Select: **F**ile from the Menu Bar

Select: **C**lose from the **F**ile drop-down menu

If you have *not* saved your file, the following dialogue box will be displayed on screen:

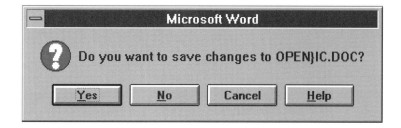

- Click on **Y**es to save the latest amendments to your document (this is usually what you want to do).
- Click on **N**o only if you are sure that you do not want to save the amendments you made after last saving the document.
- Click on **Cancel** at any time if you are not sure – you will return to the document.
- Click on **Help** at any time to read notes on options and instructions on how to operate them.

If you saved your file immediately before closing it, you will return to the Microsoft Word application window.

1.17 Exit the program if you have finished working or continue straight on to the next unit.

Exit from Word for Windows

After closing all your document files, the Microsoft Word application window is displayed on screen.

Select: **File** from the Menu Bar

Select: **Exit** from the **File** drop-down menu

Double-click on **Control button** at top left of **all windows** as you exit Windows

UNIT 2
Select text, move and copy text

At the end of Unit 2 you will have learnt how to
- *open an existing file*
- *select text*
- *delete a block of text*
- *restore deleted text*
- *move a block of text*
- *copy a block of text*
- *insert a block of text (paragraph)*

i Open an existing file

Keyboard	Mouse
Press: **Ctrl + O**	Select: **File** from the Menu Bar Select: **Open** *or* Click on the **Open** button on the Standard Tool Bar

The **Open** dialogue box is displayed on screen:

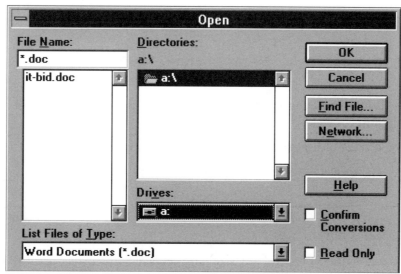

- Check that the directories and drives boxes show **a:**
- The **List Files of Type** box should show **Word Documents (*.doc)**
- A list of the files on your disk should be displayed under the **File Name** heading
- Move the pointer to the file you require and click the left button – the filename will be highlighted in blue

Click on **OK** (the file will appear on screen)

Selecting text

When you want to change a block of text in some way, it is necessary first of all to shade or highlight the particular section of text. In Word for Windows, this is called *selecting* text. The selected text shows in reverse – white letters on a black background, e.g. Selected text

To select	Keyboard	Mouse
One character (or more)	Press: **Shift** + → *or* **Shift** + ← (repeat until all required text is selected)	**Click and drag** mouse pointer across text
One word	Press: **Shift** + **Ctrl** + → *or* **Shift** + **Ctrl** + ←	**Double-click** on word
To the end of the line	Press: **Shift** + **End**	**Click and drag** mouse pointer right or down
To the beginning of the line	Press: **Shift** + **Home**	**Click and drag** mouse pointer left or up
A full line	Position pointer at beginning of line and press: **Shift** + **End** *or* Position pointer at end of line and press: **Shift** + **Home**	Position pointer in left margin (selection border) next to required line and **click**
A paragraph	—	Position pointer in selection border and **double-click** *or* Position pointer within paragraph and **triple-click**
The whole document	Press: **Ctrl** + **A**	Position pointer in selection border and **triple-click**
Any block of text	—	Position pointer at beginning of text, press: **Shift**. Then position pointer at end of text and **click**

To remove selection:
Click in any white space within document screen.

 Delete a block of text

To delete larger portions of text you *select* the block of text you wish to delete and then operate the commands for deletion:

- **Select** text to be deleted as previously described in 'Selecting text'
- Press: **Del(ete)** **Y(es)** *or* Press: ← (backspace delete key)

 Quick delete and insert text

To delete an incorrect section of text (of any size) and replace with correct text (of any size), simply select the incorrect text and key in the new text:

- Select the text to be deleted as previously described in 'Selecting text'
- Without moving the insertion point, key in the new text (the incorrect text which was initially selected will disappear)

Restore deleted text (undo)

You can restore text accidentally deleted provided that you do so straightaway. It is important that the pointer is in the correct place before you begin.

Keyboard	Mouse
Press: **Ctrl + Z**	Select: **Edit** from the Menu Bar Select: **Undo** *or* Click: Undo button on the Standard Tool Bar

Word for Windows allows you to 'undo' many previous actions. These can be accessed by clicking on the ↓ button to the right of the **Undo** button. You may like to try using this facility later in your learning program – it may be a little confusing at this stage.

 ## Move a block of text

You can move sections of text quickly without deleting and retyping. This facility is sometimes called 'cut and paste'. Text to be moved is 'cut' and placed on the 'clipboard', and then 'pasted' into its new position.

Keyboard **Mouse**

- Select: The block of text to be moved

Keyboard	Mouse
Press: **F2** Move pointer to new position Press: ↵ *or* Select: Block of text to be moved Press: **Ctrl + X** (text disappears from screen) Move pointer to new position Press: **Ctrl + V** (text reappears in its new position)	Select: **Edit** from the Menu Bar; Select: **Cut** (the text disappears from screen and is put on the clipboard) Move pointer to new position Select: **Edit** from the Menu Bar; Select: **Paste** (the text reappears in its new position) *or* Click: Cut button on Standard Tool Bar Move pointer to new position Click: Paste button on Standard Tool Bar *or* Move pointer to new position Hold down: **Ctrl** and click **right mouse button**

 ## Copy a block of text

Copying a block of text means that the text will remain in its original place in the document and a copy of the same text will also appear elsewhere. This facility is sometimes called 'copy and paste' - a copy of the text to be 'copied' is placed on the 'clipboard' and then 'pasted' into its new position.

Select the block of text to be copied:

Keyboard	Mouse
Press: **Ctrl + C**	Select: **Edit** from the Menu Bar; Select: **Copy** (the text remains on screen and a copy is put on the clipboard)
Move pointer to required position	Move pointer to required position
Press: **Ctrl + V**	Select: **Edit** from the Menu Bar; Select: **Paste** (a copy of the text appears in its required position)
	or
	Click: 📋 **Copy** button on the Standard Tool Bar
	Move pointer to new position
	Click: 📋 **Paste** button on the Standard Tool Bar

Exercise 2A

2.1 Open the file you saved in Unit 1 (filename EX1A).

2.2 Practise selecting, deleting, restoring, moving and copying blocks of text in the document on screen (EX1A) until you feel confident about the functions.

After this practice, your document may not be exactly as you saved it! Close the file without saving the changes and then open EX1A again before the next exercise.

Exercise 2B

2.3 Add your name and a heading to the top of the document as follows:

- Position the pointer at the top left of your document (the status line at the bottom of the screen should show **Ln 1 Col 10**)
- Press: ↵ twice to make two clear lines
- Press: ↑ twice to reposition pointer at top of document
- Key in: Your full name
- Press: ↵ twice to leave a clear line
- Key in: The heading **INTRODUCTION TO WORD FOR WINDOWS** (there should be one clear line between your name and heading and one clear line between the heading and the text)

2.4 Amend the document as instructed below (see also next page):

- *Delete* paragraph A (follow instructions for selecting and deleting a paragraph)
- *Restore* paragraph A (follow instructions for restoring text)
- *Delete* the circled words in paragraph B (follow instructions for selecting and deleting words)
- *Move* paragraph C so that it appears under paragraph A (follow instructions for selecting and moving a block of text)
- *Copy* the heading **INTRODUCTION TO WORD FOR WINDOWS** to E (follow instructions for selecting and copying a block of text)

Your name

INTRODUCTION TO WORD FOR WINDOWS

(A) When you start using Word for Windows, your screen will show the name of the application in the title bar at the top. Immediately below this you will see the menu bar, containing a horizontal list of words, each with the initial letter underlined.

(B) You can select an item in the menu bar by using the mouse or the keyboard. If you wish to use the mouse, you should move the mouse pointer to the required item and then 'click' the left mouse button. If you wish to use the keyboard, you should hold down the Alt key and then press the keyboard key corresponding to the initial underlined letter.

(C) The choice of keyboard or mouse operation is personal. It is generally considered that the keyboard method is faster as the operator's fingers are usually hovering over the 'QWERTY' section. However, you may prefer to use the mouse at first until you have learned all the keyboard commands. You may also find it quicker to move the insertion pointer when editing by using the mouse. Be aware of both techniques and practise them while you are learning to use the program.

(D) When you have become proficient through regular practice, you may find that you have adopted a combination of mouse and keyboard use, automatically selecting the quickest or most suitable method for the task in hand.

(E) *

2.5 You are now going to insert a new paragraph into the document.

- Position pointer at beginning of the second paragraph – the one beginning **The choice of . . .**
- Press: twice (to insert two blank lines)
- Press: ↑ twice
- Key in: The following paragraph:

The majority of functions in Word for Windows can be operated by using either the mouse or the keyboard. Clicking on an icon in the standard tool bar (below the menu bar) is probably easiest at first as the icons are easily remembered. However, there are many short-cut keyboard methods, mainly using the Ctrl key in conjunction with a keyboard character, which can save time.

2.6 Make sure there is one clear blank line above and below the paragraph you have just inserted.

2.7 Compare your work on screen with the print-out check at the back of the book. If you find any errors, correct them now.

2.8 Save your file, using filename **EX2B**.

2.9 Print a copy of your work.

2.10 Exit the program if you have finished working, or continue straight on to the next unit.

Unit 3: Change format, margins and line spacing, print preview

At the end of Unit 3 you will have learnt how to
- *change the document format in the following ways:*
  - *ragged right margin*
  - *justified right margin*
  - *inset left margin*
  - *inset right margin*
  - *double-line spacing*
- *preview a document before printing*

Formatting the right margin

Look at this paragraph – particularly at the ends of the lines. The left margin is straight, but the right margin is 'ragged' (the lines do not end at the same point). This paragraph is formatted with a *ragged* (or unjustified) right margin.

In Word for Windows you can adjust the text so that the right margin is also quite straight as shown in this paragraph. This is called a *justified* right margin (all the lines end at exactly the same point.)

It is normal practice to use either a justified right margin or a ragged right margin for a document - but not a mixture of the two formats. The left margin is normally justified. Word for Windows may be set 'by default' to a ragged or a justified right margin. You can change the default settings if required. The margin format you are currently using is displayed on screen by the alignment buttons on the Formatting Tool Bar.

You may set the right margin format you require before you key in a document. Alternatively, you may change the format during or after keying in.

Ragged (unjustified) right margin

To set the format for a document before keying in:

Keyboard	Mouse
Press: **Ctrl + L**	Select: **Format** from the Menu Bar
	Select: **Paragraph**
	Select: **Left** from the **Alignment** drop-down menu
	Click on **OK**
	or
	Click: [icon] **Align Left** button on the Standard Tool Bar

To set the format for a document after keying in:

Keyboard/mouse

Select the document (**Ctrl + A**) or the paragraph (see earlier instructions) and then operate one of the commands shown above.

Justified right margin

To set the format for a document before keying in:

Keyboard	Mouse
Press: **Ctrl + J**	Select: **Format** from the Menu Bar
	Select: **Paragraph**
	Select: **Justified** from the **Alignment** drop-down menu
	Click on **OK**
	or
	Click: [icon] **Justify** button on the Standard Tool Bar

To set the format for a document after keying in:

Keyboard/mouse

Select the document (**Ctrl + A**) or the paragraph (see earlier instructions) and then operate one of the commands shown above.

Changing left and right margins

In Word for Windows, you can change the format of a document by increasing or decreasing the margins. You can use this facility to change the margins for the whole of a document or for certain sections only.

> Insetting the margins is often used to draw the reader's attention
> to a particular piece of information – like this!

The left and right margins are usually preset at 1.25 inches or 3.17 cm. When you open a new document and request the **Normal** template, the preset (default) margins automatically come into use. Even if the text appears to fill the document window, the default margins will be used on the page when it is printed. The documents you have already printed should demonstrate this to you.

You may be given instructions to use margins in inches or in centimetres (or in both). If you change the **Units of Measurement** and make these the default settings, you can be sure of being accurate and you will not have to carry out a conversion. The unit you choose (inches or centimetres) will then be used in all relevant dialogue boxes.

Note: You may come across an instruction to change margins by, for example, 5 characters. This measurement relates to word-processing programs using 10-pitch (10 characters = 1 inch). In Word for Windows, use *inches* (5 characters = ½ inch).

Change the units of measurement

To change to inches:

- Select: **Tools** from the Menu Bar
- Select: **Options**
- Click on the **General** tab to bring this 'card' to the front
- Open the **Measurement Units** drop-down menu by clicking on the ↓
- Click on **Inches**
- Click on **OK**

To change to centimetres:

Follow instructions as above, selecting **Centimetres** in the **Measurement Units** drop-down menu.

Margins

To set margins before keying in:

Mouse/Menu Bar

Specify Page Setup:

Select: **File   Page Setup**

Click on the **Margins** tab to bring this 'card' to the front

Click on **Left** box (or move there by pressing tab key)

Key in: **Measurement required** (or use spin box to increase or decrease measurement displayed)

Click on **Right** box and repeat above

Open the **Apply To** drop-down menu by clicking on the ↓

Click on **Whole document**

Click on **OK** to operate changed margins for this document only

or

Click on **Default** to adopt these margins as the settings for the **Normal** template

Mouse/ruler markers

Display ruler on document screen:

Select: **View** from the Menu Bar

Select: **Ruler** (ruler is displayed at top of document screen)

Display tabs on ruler line:

Select: **Format** from the Menu Bar

Select: **Tabs**

Check following settings:

Default Tab Stops – 0.5 inch

Alignment – Left

Leader – None

Click on **OK**

The bottom ruler line displays the preset tab stops every $^1/_2$ inch but these are very faint. You can display the tab stops more clearly as follows:

Click on the tab-stop marker; **L** appears on the ruler line

To change the left margin:
Move the pointer to the small rectangle at the left of the ruler line
Click and drag the rectangle to the position required

To change the right margin
Move the pointer to the small triangle at the right of the ruler line
Click and drag the triangle to the position required

To change margins in an existing document:
Keyboard/mouse

Select the document (**Ctrl + A**) and then operate any of the commands shown above.

To change margins for a section of a document:
Keyboard/mouse

Select the text (as previously described) and then operate the commands shown above.

 Line spacing – single and double

In Word for Windows, you can format the text to appear in double-line spacing (i.e. one blank line between each line of text):

> This paragraph is formatted to double-line spacing, which is
>
> another method of emphasis and is used to highlight a particular
>
> portion of text.

A paragraph in double-line spacing format looks better if it has an extra line space above and below it. This 'separates' the paragraph from others in single-line spacing. An extra line space can be added or removed by using **Ctrl + 0** (zero). Pressing the keys once adds a line space; pressing the keys again deletes a line space. Use this facility to adjust the spacing above and below paragraphs to improve the appearance and legibility of your document.

Sometimes only certain portions of a document are presented in double-line spacing and this gives particular emphasis to that part of the text. Word for Windows displays double-line spacing on screen if this format has been selected but the default setting is single-line spacing.

Line spacing – single and double

To set line spacing before keying in:

Keyboard	**Mouse**
Press: **Ctrl + 2** for double-line spacing	Select: **Format** from the Menu Bar
Press: **Ctrl + 1** for single-line spacing	Select: **Paragraph**
Press: **Ctrl + 0** (zero) once to add a line space	Click on **Indents and Spacings** tab to bring this 'card' to the front
Press: **Ctrl + 0** again to delete a line space	Open the **Line Spacing** drop-down menu by clicking on the ↓
	Click on **double** or **single** (as required)

To change line spacing in an existing document:

Keyboard/mouse

Select the text (as previously described) and then operate the commands shown above.

Exercise 3A

3.1 Open the file you saved at the end of Unit 2 if it is not already on your screen. The filename is **EX2B**.

3.2 Practise using the justification facility within the document on screen. The right margin will be displayed according to the format you request.

3.3 Change the Unit of Measurement currently being used to **inches.**

3.4 Practise changing the margins in the document on screen – for the whole document and for sections of the document.

3.5 Practise changing the line spacing in the document on screen. Change the whole document, and selected paragraphs, between single and double-line spacing.

After this practice your document may not be exactly as you saved it! Close the file without saving the changes.

3.6 Reopen the file EX2B before beginning the next exercise.

Print preview

When you have made changes to the format of a document, it is useful to preview before you print. You can then check that the correct changes have been made and you can see the layout of the document as it will be when printed.

Keyboard	Mouse
Press: **Ctrl** + **F2** (a toggle switch which changes from Print Preview to Normal View)	Select: **File** from the Menu Bar Select: **Print Preview** or Click: 🔍 **Print Preview** button on the Standard Tool Bar

The **Print Preview** screen is displayed on screen: (The current page is shown in reduced size.)

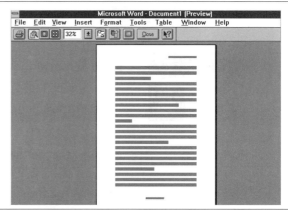

Select from the following options to view and check your document:

Type of view	Keyboard	Mouse
Normal view (the default view)	Press: **Ctrl + F2** (toggles between normal view and print preview)	Select: **View, Normal** from the Menu Bar or Click on **Normal View** on horizontal scroll bar
Page layout view (as will be printed)	—	Select: **View, Page Layout** from the Menu Bar
Print preview (shows pages in reduced size and allows editing)	Press: **Ctrl + F2** (toggles between normal view and print preview)	Select: **File, Print Preview** from the Menu Bar or Click: 🔍 **Print Preview** button on Standard Tool Bar *Note:* Click on **One Page** button 🔲 *or* **Multiple Pages** button 🔳 on Print Preview screen to view required number of pages
Zoom (magnifies part of document)	—	Click on ↓ at right of **Percentage** box on the Print Preview screen [10%] [↓] or Click: 🔍 **Magnifier** button on the Print Preview screen
Full view (menus and buttons not displayed)	—	Click: 🔲 **Full View** button on the Print Preview screen

Editing in print preview

It is possible to use the Menu Bar for some editing functions while in print preview, e.g. you may change the line spacing and justification:

Select: The **Margins** button and click and drag the margin markers to the desired positions

Printing from print preview

It is possible to print your document from the print preview screen – the whole of the current document will be printed:

Select: The **Print** button

Exercise 3B

3.7 Reformat the document as follows – refer to the instructions for changing the format of the margins and the line spacing:

- use a ragged (unjustified) right margin
- set both left and right margins at 1inch
- change the format of the second paragraph only to double-line spacing

3.8 Practise using the Print Preview screen and buttons to view and check your document, comparing it with the print-out for EX3B at the back of the book.

If your layout is correct, proceed to the next step. If your layout is not correct, reread the instructions for formatting to get the layout right. You can edit your work within the Print Preview screen or you can return to normal view to do this.

3.9 Save your file using filename **EX3B**.

3.10 Print a copy of your work.

Exercise 3C

3.11 Reformat the document you have just printed as follows:

- use the fully justified format (left and right margins justified)
- inset both margins by ½ inch (5 characters)
- use double-line spacing for the fourth paragraph only

3.12 Print preview your document comparing it with the print-out for EX3C at the back of the book.

If your layout is correct, proceed to the next step. If your layout is not correct, reread the instructions for formatting to get the layout right. You can edit your work within the print preview screen or you can return to normal view to do this.

3.13 Save your file using filename **EX3C**.

3.14 Print a copy of your work.

3.15 Exit the program if you have finished working or continue straight on to the next unit.

Find (search) and replace text, spelling tool

At the end of Unit 4 you will have learnt how to
- *find (search) and replace text in a document*
- *spellcheck a document*
- *spellcheck a block of text*

 ## Find (search) and replace

In word processing it is possible to find automatically a given word or phrase and exchange it for another given word throughout a document. An example of the way in which this function could be used is a letter being sent out from school to parents. It would be very easy to produce some letters that referred to 'your son' and some that referred to 'your daughter', or every occurrence of 'he' could be changed to 'she'.

You can use Word's find and replace function in two different ways (the first method is the safer in examinations):

1. You can ask Word to stop every time it has located the 'find' word and wait for your confirmation before it 'replaces' the word (**Replace**). If you find an entry that you do not wish to be changed, you can skip over it and move to the next occurrence of the search (**Find Next**)

2. You can allow Word to go straight through the document 'finding and replacing' without stopping for confirmation from you (**Replace All**).

Find (search) and replace text

Keyboard	**Mouse and menu**
Press **Ctrl + H**	Select: **E**dit, **R**eplace

- In the **Find What** box, key in the text to be searched for
- In the **Replace With** box, key in the replacement text
- From the **Search** box, choose **All**, **Down** or **Up**:

    All   – search through all the document

    Down – search from insertion point to end of document

    Up   – search from insertion point to start of document

Select from the find and replace dialogue buttons as appropriate:

Button	Action
Replace	Allows control over each replacement one at a time
Find Next	Skips an entry which you do not wish to be changed and moves to the next occurrence of the search
Replace All	Replaces all occurrences automatically

Optional facilities:

- From **Special** or **Format** options, select any special characteristics to find if appropriate
- Select **Match Case** – to find the exact combination of upper-case and lower-case letters entered in the find-what box
- Select **Find Whole Words Only** – to find occurrences that are not part of a larger word (e.g. the word *rate* could appear in i*rate*, c*rate* and desec*rate*d)

Press: **Esc** to finish   Select: **Cancel** to finish

Find text

If you only want to *find* text (without replacing it), similar commands can be accessed through the **Find** dialogue box. Select **Edit**, **Find** from the menu or press: **Ctrl + F**

Tip: Sometimes you can't see the text under the dialogue box so you can't decide whether to replace or not! Using the mouse, point to the middle of the horizontal blue bar running across the top of the dialogue box and drag the box down to bottom left or right of screen.

Exercise 4A

4.1 Retrieve the file **EX1A** from your disk and, using the find and replace function, change **letter** to **character** in the first and second paragraphs.

4.2 Change the format of the document as follows:
- justified right margin
- inset both margins by ½ inch

4.3 Preview the file to check the format changes. Save and print your document using filename **EX4A**. Check your print-out with that at the back of the book. If you find any errors, correct them on screen, save your document again and print again if necessary.

Exercise 4B

4.4 Retrieve the file **EX2A** from your disk. Using the find and replace function, change **using** to **operating** in the second and third paragraphs.

4.5 Change the format of the document as follows:
- justified right margin
- double-line spacing for second paragraph
- inset left margin only by ½ inch

4.6 Preview the file to check the format changes. Save and print your document using filename **EX4B**. Check your print-out with that at the back of the book. If you find any errors, correct them on screen, save your document again and print again if necessary.

Spelling check

Word for Windows has a built-in spelling check facility. The spellcheck memory contains thousands of words, but doesn't include many proper names (e.g. cities, surnames, etc.) or some acceptable abbreviations (e.g. VDU). If you were going to use an unusual word fairly frequently that is not already in the spellcheck memory, you have an option to *add* it to the list. Spellcheck would never stop on that word again.

Automatic spellchecking is very useful and you should always 'run spellcheck' before you save or print a file, but you must also proof-read the text yourself. The spellcheck facility simply compares each word you have keyed in with its own 'dictionary' of words. If you have keyed in the wrong version of a word, e.g. **their** instead of **there**, spellcheck will not detect this as both versions are spelt correctly.

Only you can tell if you have copied names of people or places correctly and if a piece of information you were asked to find is correct.

Spelling tool

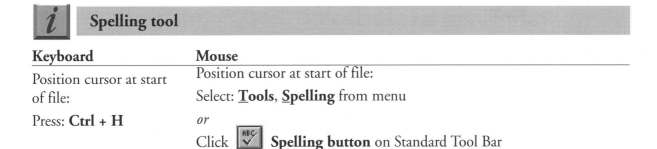

The **Spelling** dialogue box is displayed on screen:

- Spellcheck displays any misspelt word in the **Not in Dictionary** box
- Word displays the most obvious replacement in the **Change To** box
- You may, however, select one of the alternatives shown in the **Suggestions** box
- You can also edit the text yourself in the **Change To** box if this is more appropriate, e.g. if you have missed the space between two words

Select from the spelling dialogue buttons as appropriate:

Button	Action
Ignore	Leaves the word unchanged the first time it occurs but stops on it whenever it occurs again
Ignore all	Leaves the word unchanged on every occurrence (until you restart Word)
Change	Accepts the spelling in the **Change To** box or the **Suggestions** box
Change All	Changes the first and all subsequent occurrences of the misspelt word
Add	Adds the word to the Custom Dictionary in the **Add Words To** box
AutoCorrect	Adds the misspelt word and its correction to the AutoCorrect list – i.e. if you ever misspell this word in the same way again as you are typing, Word will correct it automatically for you!
Press: **Esc** to finish	Select: **Cancel** to finish

Tip: If you do not wish to check the spelling of the whole document, you can first select/highlight a portion of text or even one word before running spellcheck.

4.7 Start a new file. Key in the following text – retain all the deliberate spelling and keying-in mistakes (these have been circled) for the purpose of this exercise:

THE CASTLE OF KNOSSOS

It is the largest of the four castles on the island of (crete) to have been (exscavated). It covers an area of 22,000 (squaremiles) and is (vseerla) storeys (hiph.)

The castle was discovered by the English (archaellogist), Arthur Evans, who worked with deep scholarly knowledge and enthusiasm to bring to (lite) the most perfect and (impresive) creation of Minoan (arkitecture.)

Extraordinary works of art were uncovered, astonishing the (wholeworld.) Statuettes of precious materials, (outsnading) stone ritual (vesells), splendid paintings and other admirable objects were unearthed between 1900-1935.

4.8 Move the cursor to the top of the document and run the spellcheck facility.

The word **KNOSSOS** will be queried – this is because the word is not in the spellcheck dictionary although it is not necessarily spelt incorrectly. Check that you have copied the word correctly. If so, select **Ignore**.

The word **crete** will be queried – this is because the word should have an initial capital as shown in the **Change To** box. Select **Change**.

The word **exscavated** should be queried – this time the word is definitely spelt wrongly. Word offers a replacement in the **Change To** box. Select **Change**.

The text **squaremiles** is queried because there is no space between the two words. Edit the text within the **Change To** box and then select **Change**.

The word **vseerlal** is queried - the word is so badly spelt that Word is unable to offer any suitable replacement. In the **Change To** box, delete the text and type in the correct word **several.** Select **Change**.

The word **hiph** is queried. Select the replacement word **high** from the **Suggestions** box. Select **Change**.

4.9 Continue with spellcheck, either accepting or replacing text as appropriate.

4.10 Replace the word **castle** with **palace** throughout the document.

4.11 Save and print your document using filename **EX4C.** Check your print-out with that at the back of the book. If you find any errors, correct them on screen, save your document again and print again if necessary.

4.12 Exit the program if you have finished working or continue straight on to the next unit.

Unit 5: Formatting/emphasizing text

At the end of Unit 5 you will have learnt how to
- *embolden text, before typing and during editing*
- *underline text, before typing and during editing*
- *centre text, before typing and during editing*
- *format text by changing the font typeface and point size*

Formatting/emphasizing text

You have already practised using CAPITALS, inset margins and double-line spacing as methods of text emphasis. In Word for Windows, formatted/emphasized text is seen on screen as it will appear when printed on paper. Some additional methods of formatting or emphasizing text are:

Bold type (heavy print to make it look darker) is a method of emphasizing words or phrases (especially headings) to make them look more noticeable and to stress their importance to the reader.

<u>Underline</u> is used in a similar way to embolden for text emphasis.

Italic can also be used to emphasize text – it is more commonly used within the main body of the document.

CENTRED TEXT

Centring of text, particularly headings, emphasizes the text. Main headings are often centred while subheadings are typed at the left margin. The centring function is useful when preparing certain documents such as menus, where an attractive display is important.

Font typeface: Another way of emphasizing the text would be to change the font typeface. For example:

> **This sentence is typed in Times Bold**
>
> `This sentence is typed in Courier Italic`

Font point size: The default point size of text for word-processed documents is usually 10 or 12 points. The actual size of the printed text, however, is relevant to the typeface being used – even if you select the same point size for different fonts they will not always appear as the same size. For example:

> This sentence is typed in 10-point
> (Adobe Garamond Typeface)
>
> This sentence is typed in 10-point
> (Helvetica typeface)

You could use a larger point size for subheadings or main headings in a document, or even a different font. It is not considered good practice to use more than one typeface within the same document, although several point sizes of the same font typeface are acceptable.

FORMATTING/EMPHASIZING TEXT 35

You may be asked to remove text formatting/emphasis, e.g. changing text from bold to normal type, removing underline, etc.

Formatting/emphasizing text

Format/emphasis	Keyboard	Mouse	
Bold	Press: **Ctrl + B**	Click: Bold button	**B**
Italics	Press: **Ctrl + I**	Click: *I*talics button	*I*
<u>Underline</u>	Press: **Ctrl + U**	Click: <u>U</u>nderline button	<u>U</u>
Centre text	Press: **Ctrl + E**	Click: Centre button	≡
Change font	Press: **Ctrl + Shift + F** Select a font from the list	Click: Font button Select a font from the list	Roman ▼

Change font size
   Next larger point size
   Next smaller point size
	Press: **Ctrl + Shift + P**
	Press: **Ctrl + >**
	Press: **Ctrl + <**
		Click: Font size button
		Select a point size from the list
			10 ▼

Remove text emphasis/ back to plain text	Select text to change back: Press: **Ctrl + SPACEBAR**	Select text to change back: Click: Appropriate button	

To format text while typing:
- Operate the appropriate command (e.g. click on the **B** button to switch bold text on)
- Key in the text
- Operate the command again to switch the emphasis off

To format existing text:
- elect the text to be changed
- Operate the appropriate command

Exercise 5A

5.1 Starting a new file:

Click: **B** bold button on the Formatting Tool Bar

Type: **This sentence is typed in bold.**

Click: the **B**old button again to stop bold

Press: ↵

Click: <u>U</u> underline button on the Formatting Tool Bar

Type: <u>This sentence is typed with underline.</u>

Click: the <u>U</u>(nderline) button again to stop underline

Press: ↵

Click: ≡ centre button on the Formatting Tool Bar

Type: **This sentence is centred.**

Press: ↵ (text should now be centred on screen)

Click: The left-align button to return text to the left margin

5.2 Choose a different font style from the selection shown in the font box on the Formatting Tool Bar and apply this to the first sentence.

5.3 Choose a different point size from the selection shown in the font size box on the Formatting Tool Bar and apply this to the last sentence.

5.4 Delete the text on your screen – you do not need to save or print your work.

Exercise 5B

5.5 Starting a new file, practise combining methods of text formatting/emphasis by keying in the following short menu. Each line should be centred, with bold and/or underline being added where shown. You may choose a different font style for the main heading only.

<u>SANCHA'S BISTRO</u>

<u>MENU</u>

Soup of the Day
Prawn Cocktail
Mushrooms in Garlic Sauce

Chicken Orientale
Somerset Pork in Cider
Poached Halibut in White Wine Sauce

Lemon Meringue Pie
Fresh Strawberries and Cream
Assorted Cheese and Pickles with Biscuits

Choice of boiled or roast potatoes and fresh vegetables with all main meals.

5.6 Save and print your document using filename **EX5B**. Check your printout with the example above and correct any errors if necessary.

Exercise 5C

5.7 Starting a new file, key in the following exercise, using bold, underline and centring where shown.

GARDEN WALLS

<u>BRICKS</u>

There are literally <u>hundreds</u> of different bricks available but not all of them are suitable for use in the garden.

Common bricks - fairly dull and uninteresting in appearance.

Facing bricks - have an attractive appearance and are usually the ones used for the outsides of homes. A wide variety of <u>colours</u> and <u>textures</u> is available, some of which weather better than others. Many facing bricks have the special appearance only onto three of the four brick faces which could pose a problem.

Engineering bricks - particularly <u>dense</u>, <u>strong</u> and <u>water resistant</u>. They are sometimes used for brickwork below ground level, damp-proof courses or in a soil-retaining wall.

5.8 Save your document using filename **EX5C**.
(There is no need to print your work at this stage.)

Exercise 5D

5.9 Add more text emphasis to the document you have just keyed in:
- Centre the subheading **BRICKS**
- Change the emphasis from underline to italics for the word **hundreds** in the first sentence.
- Change the emphasis from underline to bold for all circled words
- Add underline to all the words underlined with - - - - as shown in the copy below.

GARDEN WALLS

<u>BRICKS</u>

There are literally <u>hundreds</u> of different bricks available but not all of them are suitable for use in the garden.

Common bricks - fairly dull and uninteresting in appearance.

Facing bricks - have an attractive appearance and <u>are</u> usually the ones used for the outsides of homes. A wide variety of colours and textures is available, some of which weather better than others. many facing bricks have the special appearance only onto three of the four brick faces which could pose a problem.

Engineering bricks - particularly dense, strong and water resistant they are sometimes used for brickwork below ground level, damp-proof courses or in a soil-retaining wall.

5.10 Save and print your document using filename **EX5D**. Check your print-out with that at the back of the book. If you find any errors, retrieve the document and correct.

Exercise 5E

5.11 Retrieve the file you saved as EX5D (unless it is already on screen) and delete *all* the text emphasis throughout the whole document (i.e. bold, underline, centring).

5.12 Check carefully to ensure that all emphasis is removed and that the whole document appears in normal type only. There is no need to print your work.

5.13 Exit the program if you have finished working or continue straight on to the next unit.

Consolidation 1

Exercise 6A

6.1 Load your program and, starting a new file, key in the following text using a left-aligned format (i.e. ragged right margin). Don't forget to type your full name at the top of the document.

ROCK GARDENS

A rock garden is basically an arrangement of rocks encompassing a collection of alpine and other small plants. The rocks should be set out in a non-uniform manner in order to resemble a natural rock outcrop. There should be little earth showing and an abundance of plant life thriving in conditions reflecting their natural habitat.

The growing medium should be suitable for alpine plants, with just sufficient moisture in summer and very good drainage and protection from lying damp in winter.

Moisture loss from the thin earth in the rock garden can be reduced to some extent by a covering of fine gravel.

It is always useful to visit a few rock gardens before planning your own layout. Study them carefully and consider what is entailed. Remember that, once established, the rock garden is a more or less permanent feature - so it makes good sense to put some thought into it and get it right first time.

The cost will largely depend on your alpines, the local availability of suitable stone, access by lorries, and general handling costs.

6.2 Use the spellcheck facility to check your work for spelling errors.

6.3 Compare your work *on screen* with the printed text above. Proof-read carefully and make any necessary amendments.

6.4 Save and print your document using filename **EX6A**. Check your print-out with the printed exercise above. If you find any errors, make the necessary corrections.

Exercise 6B

6.5 Retrieve EX6A if it is not already on your screen.

6.6 On the first line insert the word **informal** before **arrangement.** In the last paragraph, insert the words **choice of** before **alpines.**

6.7 Delete the paragraph beginning **Moisture loss from…**

6.8 Insert the following paragraph after the second paragraph:

Many alpine plants have long roots which penetrate deep into rock crevices and into damp patches of earth under and behind rocks.

6.9 In the paragraph beginning **The growing medium…**, insert **for their needs** following the word **moisture**.

In the first line of the paragraph change **basically** to **essentially**.

6.10 In the paragraph beginning **Many alpine plants...**, delete **damp patches** and replace with **moist pockets**.

6.11 Reformat the document to
- first paragraph only in double-line spacing
- justified right margin
- inset both margins by ½ inch

6.12 Centre, enbolden and underline the heading.

6.13 Move the fifth paragraph, which begins **It is always useful...** so that it becomes the last paragraph.

6.14 Replace the word **earth** with **soil** wherever it occurs (twice in all).

6.15 Save and print your document using filename **EX6B**. Check your print-out with that at the back of the book. If you find any errors, retrieve the document and correct.

6.16 Exit the program if you have finished working or clear your screen and continue straight on to the next exercise.

Exercise 6C

6.17 Open a file and input the following text with an unjustified right margin and a justified left margin:

TRAVELLING BY AIR WITH YOUNG INFANTS

An airport delay is fraught for everyone, but with young infants can be quite traumatic. If you are planning to travel abroad by air, go prepared!

Make up a child's pack of time-consuming games, books, puzzles, pens and colouring pencils. Include a treat such as the child's favourite packet of sweets or a drink. There are a number of travel games available nowadays in the shops which are specially designed for playing 'en route'. Some of these have special magnetic playing boards to prevent pieces from being lost.

Pack enough food and drink in hand luggage to allow for delay en route.

Don't forget several changes of nappy if you are travelling with a baby. Most UK airports have a mother and baby room to make changing and feeding less of a hassle.

If travelling with babies or small infants a collapsible pushchair is a must. Try to keep it with you on the plane rather than checking it in with the luggage.

Loose-fitting garments (such as cotton tracksuits) in layers that can be peeled on and off as the temperature varies are the most suitable clothing. Trainer type trackshoes, however, can be hot.

6.18 Use the spellcheck facility to check your work for spelling errors.

6.19 Compare your work *on screen* with the printed text above. Proof-read carefully and make any necessary amendments.

6.20 Save and print your document using filename **EX6C**. Check your print-out with the printed exercise in this unit. If you find any errors, make the necessary corrections.

Exercise 6D

6.21 Retrieve EX6C if it is not already on your screen.

6.22 On the first line insert the word **interminable** before **airport**. In the first paragraph, insert the words **expect the worst and** before **go prepared!**

6.23 Delete the paragraph beginning **If travelling with babies...**

6.24 Insert the following paragraph after the second paragraph:

Pass some time in the spectator gallery watching planes land and take off.

6.25 In the paragraph beginning **Make up a child's...**, insert **special** before **treat**.

Replace **en route** with **on the move**.

6.26 Reformat the document to:

- second paragraph only in double-line spacing
- justified right margin
- inset both margins by ½ inch

6.27 Move the last paragraph beginning **Loose fitting garments ...**so it becomes the second.

6.28 Replace the words **infants** with **children**.

6.29 Centre and embolden the heading.

6.30 Save and print your document using filename **EX6D**. Check your print-out with that at the back of the book. If you find any errors, retrieve the document and correct.

6.31 Exit the program if you have finished working or clear your screen and continue straight on to the next unit.

UNIT 7 *Examination practice 1*

This examination practice unit is for RSA CLAIT Word Processing.

Exercise 7A

7.1 Start up your word-processing system, open a new file and key in the following text:

BREAD IS GOOD FOR YOUR FITNESS

Contrary to popular belief, bread is not a fattening food. Instead, it provides protein, vitamins and minerals essential for proper fitness and many fitness experts actually recommend increasing the amount of fibre-rich foods like bread into our diets. It is the fat you spread on bread that makes it fattening.

The baking of bread has progressed a lot since its early days when coarse flour was mixed with water and then dried in the sun, producing a very heavy unleavened bread.

There is a wide variety of breads available - white, wholemeal, rye, granary etc. It also comes in a variety of appearances - sliced or unsliced loaves, rolls, muffins, bagels, croissants. Nowadays, bread can be enjoyed in many delicious ways.

To keep bread fresher, store it at room temperature in a clean well-ventilated container. Putting bread in the refrigerator makes it stale more quickly. However, bread freezes very well and can be toasted from frozen. Bread cubes and crumbs can be prepared in advance and frozen until required.

7.2 Proof-read your work, correct errors, save and print a copy of the document using an unjustified right-hand margin. (Use filename **EX7A**.)

7.3 In the first paragraph, replace the words **essential for proper** with **necessary for good**.

Insert the word **starchy** after the word **fibre-rich**.

7.4 In the paragraph beginning **There is a wide variety…**, delete the sentence beginning **Nowadays, bread can be enjoyed…**

7.5 Insert the following paragraph after the paragraph beginning **Contrary to popular…**

The type of flour used dictates the colour, flavour and texture of the bread. Most bread in England is made from wheat flour – wholemeal is considered to be a 'fitness' food as it has nothing added or taken away from the original grain, brown usually contains 85% of the original grain since most of the bran and germ are removed, and white usually contains 75% of the grain.

7.6 Delete the paragraph beginning **The baking of bread has progressed...**

7.7 Centre and embolden the heading.

7.8 Set in the whole document by ½ inch on each side and justify the text.

7.9 Change the second paragraph only to double-line spacing.

7.10 Move the third paragraph beginning **There is a wide variety...** so that it becomes the last paragraph.

7.11 Replace the word **fitness** with the word **health** wherever it occurs (four times in all).

7.12 Save and print one copy. (Use filename **EX7B**.) Ensure that the document is saved on disk and close down the system.

UNIT 8 Unfamiliar and foreign words

At the end of Unit 8 you will have learnt how to
- *reproduce unfamiliar and foreign words correctly, copying the spelling exactly as shown*
- *proof-read your work carefully*

Text containing unfamiliar or foreign words

Each branch of commerce and each industry has its own vocabulary or 'jargon'.

It is vital that you take extra care when you are keying in words which are not familiar to you. If you come across a word which is new to you at work, note how it is spelt and copy it exactly, letter for letter. If you think the word is likely to crop up again, make a note of it. You should take particular care with the names of people or organizations, addresses, amounts of money, etc. It is a good idea to keep a note of regular contacts or clients.

Proof-reading is very important with unfamiliar material. Check your work carefully yourself and, if possible, ask colleagues to check the work too. You could do the same for them!

Commonly used words can be added to the spelling dictionary in Word for Windows so that they will be checked during the spellcheck process. Don't forget to use the spelling tool after each piece of work which you complete before you save and print.

Exercise 8A

8.1 Starting a new file, key in the following text, copying the unfamiliar words carefully:

WINDOW BOXES AND HANGING BASKETS

The compost should be a compound of sterilized soil and peat, with a proprietary fertilizer. Extra feeding with a granular or liquid fertilizer, preferably organic, will be imperative. Wood and plastic are good construction materials: wire should be galvanized or plastic coated.

Array according to height and habit. Trailing plants such as nasturtiums, geraniums, thunbergia and campanula isophylla should be placed in the foreground or sides. Bushy specimens are best placed centrally - look for alyssum, begonia, impatiens and iberis.

The colours of the blooms should be considered and most people favour a variety of brilliant shades to brighten a dismal wall or a drab street window. Foliage can be utilised to great effect in this respect with variegated leaves being very popular.

Take pains not to overfeed and preclude dehydration by watering two or three times weekly. Renew exhausted soil systematically to ensure success and to minimise the risk of disease and infestation.

8.2 Format the document as follows:
- justified margins
- left and right margins of 1.5 inches
- double spacing for whole document

8.3 Save and print your work using filename **EX8A**. Check your print-out with that at the back of the book. If you find any errors, correct them and save your document again. Print again if necessary.

Exercise 8B

8.4 Starting a new file, key in the following text, copying the unfamiliar words carefully:

THE POLITICAL AND ADMINISTRATIVE SYSTEM IN FRANCE

France is divided into 22 regions, each comprising up to five 'departements'. These departements are made up of smaller units called 'communes'. Elected representatives are grouped into 'conseils' at each level. A president presides over a regional counseil and a 'maire' leads a commune. These leaders have substantial influence as they are frequently also members of parliament in the 'assemblee nationale' or in the 'senat'.

Companies in France are classified according to the number of employees and not according to their mode of ownership. Companies contracting up to 500 people are known as 'petites et moyennes entreprises'. Few concerns are greater than this, the majority having between 10 and 100 employees. There remains a large number of associations still controlled by founding families and privately owned. However, France also has one of the largest nationalised sectors in Western Europe, ranging from banking and insurance to aluminium, aerospace and chemicals.

The French are extraordinarily legalistic and function within an environment of complex, contradictory and incomprehensible laws. The paradox arises in the French delectation in flouting the law! Seemingly over-bureaucratic procedures are obligatory when conducting business in France and managers are often products of the prestigious business and engineering colleges which exist alongside the universities, and to which entry is arduous.

8.5 Format the document as follows:
- ragged right margin
- left and right margins of 1.75 inches
- double spacing for last paragraph only

8.6 Save and print your work using filename **EX8B**. Check your print-out with that at the back of the book. If you find any errors, correct them and save your document again. Print again if necessary.

UNIT 9 *Text editing, grammar tool*

At the end of Unit 9 you will have learnt how to
- amend text in accordance with common text-correction signs
- expand correctly common abbreviations
- amend uncorrected typographical errors
- amend uncorrected errors of agreement
- use the spelling and grammar tools to check text before printing

i Typescript containing correction signs

A word-processor operator is seldom given work which simply requires to be copied exactly as it is. A photocopier could do the job much more quickly! Usually, the 'copy' (text which the operator copies from) contains amendments.

Examples

This sentence has been changed. *(amended)*

should be keyed in as **This sentence has been amended.**

Please delete or ~~omit~~ this word.

should be keyed in as **Please delete this word.**

Extra words should be inserted for /to make sense. *(this sentence)*

should be keyed in as **Extra words should be inserted for this sentence to make sense.**

You may be asked to move words or sentences or phrases.

should be keyed in as **You may be asked to move sentences or words or phrases.**

Exercise 9A

9.1 Starting a new file, key in the following text making all the necessary amendments as you go along:

> SERVICE TO TEACHERS AND LECTURERS
>
> The Education Resource Service offers a wide range of materials covering all aspects of the history and progress of technology in the chemical industry. Our aim is to give students and pupils a better understanding of the way that technology affects their everyday lives.
>
> In addition to a comprehensive range of booklets, resource packs, videos, worksheets and training notes, guidance is given on the National Curriculum. The materials are suited to all ages and are divided by Key Stages.
>
> A new initiative being developed within the Service in conjunction with other agencies, is that of teacher placement. The rapid rate of change means that it is vital that our educators are equipped to deal with projects related to current industrial practice and the new placement scheme hopes to assist in this.

9.2 Press ↵ several times to leave a space before the next exercise.

Typescript containing abbreviations

Text authors often use abbreviations when writing out copy which is to be processed by a word-processor operator. In the work situation, you would quickly get used to individual authors' 'shorthand'.

The following list shows some abbreviations you can expect to come across in basic examinations such as RSA's Core Text Processing Skills:

accom.	accommodation	recom.	recommend
advert(s).	advertisement(s)	ref(s).	reference(s)
bel.	believe	resp.	responsible
bus.	business	sec(s).	secretary/ies
co(s).	company/ies	sep.	separate
def.	definitely	thro'	through
necy.	necessary	sh.	shall
opp(s).	opportunity(ies)	wh.	which
rec.	receive	w.	with
recd.	received		

Note: The full stop is used after the abbreviation to show that the word is shortened. You should not type the full stop (unless the word is at the end of a sentence, of course).

You will also be expected to key in the following in full:
- days of the week, e.g. Wednesday, Thursday
- months of the year, e.g. February, September
- words in addresses, e.g. Grove, Drive, Crescent
- complimentary closes, e.g. Yours faithfully/sincerely

Don't forget that you should use the spelling tool before you save and print each document.

Exercise 9B

9.3 Key in the following text, typing all the abbreviations in full as you go along:

BOOKING YOUR HOLIDAY

When you read the adverts. in the newspapers, you will feel that you def. need a holiday. The small adverts. ask you to telephone or to write for more details. You will then rec. a brochure for each sep. co. wh. is advertising. Flicking thro' the leaflets w. their glossy pictures will encourage you to bel. that each destination is the best - the choice is difficult.

Before booking your accom., check that the co. concerned is a member of an organisation resp. for maintaining standards within the industry. Such an organisation would recom. that only such a bus. should be used. Take the opp. to discuss your requirements w. an agent and w. friends. A good ref. from someone else can put your mind at rest.

9.4 Proof-read your work carefully, comparing it with the print-out at the back of the book. If you find any errors, correct them. Use the spelling tool to check that you have expanded the abbreviations correctly.

9.5 Save your document using filename **EX9B** and print one copy.

Typescript containing typographical errors

Text processing may involve putting right any mistakes made in previous print-outs. Watch out for uncorrected spelling errors and transposition errors.

Examples

This sentance contains 3 speling errers.

should be keyed in as: **This** *sentence* contains 3 *spelling errors*.

This sentence contians 2 transpositoin errors.

should be keyed in as: **This sentence** *contains* 2 *transposition errors*.

In the RSA Core Text Processing Skills examination, any words which are incorrect will be circled. It is up to you to decide what is wrong and to key in the word correctly.

Exercise 9C

9.6 Starting a new file, key in the following text, correcting all the words which are circled as you go along:

FRENCH POLISHING

This method of treating wood gives the best finnish for furniture. the method was intorduced into europe in the sixtenth century and was developped by a French cabinet maker in the early nineteenth centurey.

Wood can only be stianed to a darker shade. If a lighter shade is reqired it must be bleached w. a wood bleech and then stained. Preparatoin off the surface is extremly important as flaws become more apparant under French Polish.

Wax and greese can be removed w. white sprit and fine steal wool but a very bad finish may need stripping completly.

9.7 Proof-read your work carefully, comparing it with the print-out at the back of the book. If you find any errors, correct them. Use the spelling tool to check that you have spelt the words correctly.

9.8 Save your document as **EX9C** and close the file. There is no need to print at this stage.

Typescript containing errors of agreement

As you are keying in text, you should make sure that what you are typing makes sense. You should watch out for errors of agreement when the noun and the verb in a sentence do not agree.

Examples

This class of girls are irritating.

should be keyed in as **This class of girls is irritating** (because there is only *one* class). If there were more than one class, you would key in: **These classes of girls are irritating**.

The difference between the two word-processing programs were demonstrated by the supervisor

should be keyed in as **The difference between the two word-processing programs was demonstrated by the supervisor** (because there are *two* programs but only *one* difference).

Grammar tool

Word will check your file for possible grammar and style errors and offer suggestions for correcting them. The grammar tool will also identify spelling errors and automatically 'toggle' into the spelling tool if necessary. If you know your grammar is weak, this is a useful facility, but still does not replace personal proof-reading skills.

The grammar check facility should be used with caution since it may prompt you to make significant changes to another author's copy. This may not be acceptable to the text author, and changes of that nature should *not* be used when copying from an examination paper, when the copy must be followed exactly.

Grammar tool

Mouse/menu

Select: **Tools Grammar**

The **Grammar** dialogue box is displayed on screen:

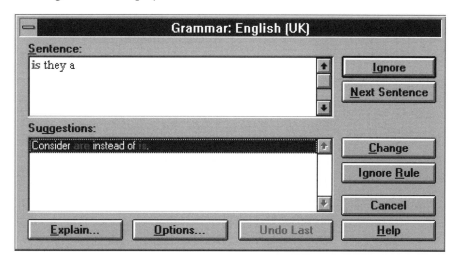

- Grammar check displays any sentences which may require correction in the **Sentence** box. You can choose to correct the item in the box or in the document
- Word displays the suggested correction in the **Suggestions** box

Select from the grammar dialogue buttons as appropriate:

Button	Action
Ignore	Leaves the marked text unchanged the first time it occurs but stops on it whenever it occurs again
Ignore Rule	Leaves the marked text unchanged on every occurrence
Next Sentence	Moves to next sentence with a grammatical error
Change	Makes the correction selected in the **Sentence** box
Delete	Carries out any deletions made in the **Sentence** box

Optional facilities

- Select **Explain** for an explanation of why the marked text may not be grammatically correct
- Select **Options** to specify rules for Word to use when checking grammar
- Select **Undo Last** to reverse the most recent action made during the current grammar-checking session

Press: **Esc** to finish   Select: **Cancel** to finish

Exercise 9D

9.9 Starting a new file, key in the following text - retain all the deliberate grammatical mistakes (these have been circled) for the purpose of this exercise:

COOKING TIPS FOR PASTA

Cooking pasta is quick and eas*y* -a*s* easy as boiled potato*es* , *b*ut with no peeling to d*o* ! When the salted water *are* boiling, add the pasta gently.

9.10 Move the cursor to the top of the file and run the grammar checking facility:

The *dash* before the words **as easy** is highlighted in red. Word prompts you to use consistent spacing around the punctuation mark. In the **Sentence** box, use normal editing procedures to insert a space to the right of the dash. Select **Change**.

The *comma* after the word **potatoes** is highlighted in red. Word prompts you to delete the space before this punctuation mark. In the **Sentence** box, use normal editing procedures to delete the space before the comma. Select **Delete**.

The *exclamation mark* after the words **to do** is highlighted in red. Word prompts you to delete the space before this punctuation mark. In the **Sentence** box, use normal editing procedures to delete the space before the exclamation mark. Select **Delete**.

In the last sentence, Word prompts you to choose 1) **waters** instead of **water** or 2) **is** instead of **are**. From the **Suggestions** box, select the second option. Select **Change**.

9.11 Close this file *without* saving.

Exercise 9E

9.12 Open the file you saved earlier – EX9C – and key in the following text, correcting the circled words as you go along:

PIZZA PRONTO

In this country, everyone *tend* to think of Italian food in terms of take-away pizzas and ready-made lasagnes, but traditional cooking in Italy normally *demand* hours of preparation. Meals rarely *consists* of one course only.

Although fresh pasta has a much better *tastes* than the dried variety, making the dough, wh. then needs rolling and cutting, *take* hours. The pace of modern life, especially in the northern cities, *mean* that the use of bottled and canned sauces *are* increasing.

If the basic *ingredient* of pastas, herbs and sauces are of good quality, then perhaps the results will be acceptable - at least for weekdays.

9.13 Proof-read your work carefully, comparing it with the print-out at the back of the book. If you find any errors, correct them. Use the grammar tool to check that you have amended the text correctly.

9.14 Save your work as **EX9E** and print a copy.

9.15 Exit the program if you have finished working or continue straight on to the next unit.

UNIT 10 Working from manuscript copy

At the end of Unit 10 you will have practised keying in text from copy which is hand written and contains amendments and corrections.

i Typing from manuscript copy

'Manuscript' means written by hand. Word-processor operators are often given work in hand-written form.

When keying in from a hand-written draft, make sure you can read *all* the words written in longhand. If any words are not clear, *look for the same letter formations* in other parts of the draft where they may be more legible. If you still have difficulty, read the document for context to try to get the sense of it.

The standard correction signs and abbreviations which you learnt in the previous unit will appear in manuscript copy as well as in typescript.

Exercise 10A

10.1 Key in the following text, using a ragged right margin and double-line spacing:

THE HOMOEOPATHIC ALTERNATIVE ← underline

At the beginning of the 19th century, a German physician named Samuel Hahnemann introduced a more gentle methods of treating the common diseases and ailments of the time. He used natural substances of plant, mineral and animal origin. The effectiveness of the remedies was proved thro' the treatment of malaria w. Quinine bark.

The approach and attitudes to the patient established in the early days have remained the same. ~~although treatments~~ All the factors affecting the patient are considered - both emotional and physical. A remedy is chosen not only to fit the symptoms but also to suit the ~~patient~~ individual and his/her lifestyle. Homoeopathy def. suits the modern approach to medicine where the patient wants to be involved in and take more responsibility for their own well-being.

10.2 Use the spelling tool and then proof-read your work carefully comparing it with the print-out at the back of the book. If you find any errors, correct them.

10.3 Save your work using filename **EX10A** and print one copy.

Additional text correction signs

You have already learnt basic correction signs in Unit 9. Look at the following examples of other signs which you may see on typewritten or manuscript text:

// *or* [

Start a new paragraph where you see either of these signs. The letters NP (new paragraph) may also appear in the margin.

The 'run on' sign is used when two paragraphs should be joined together.

To join two paragraphs, move the pointer to the first character of the second paragraph and press the backspace delete key twice.

If you see a tick inside a circle in the margin, look for a word (or words) in the text which has a dotted line underneath it. These two signs mean that you should insert the word with the dotted line underneath, even though it may have been crossed out. The word 'stet' is sometimes written in the margin instead of the tick in the circle.

(✓) When you type this sentence, ins~~delete~~ert this word.

should be typed as **When you type this sentence, insert this word.**

⌊ word 1 ⌊word 2 ⌉   This sign means that you should type word 2 before word 1. This is called transposition.

Two words in ⌊sentence ⌈this⌉ are the wrong way round.

should be typed as **Two words in this sentence are the wrong way round.**

You may also have to transpose words vertically, for example if they are in a list.

Dot Matrix	*should be typed as*	Dot Matrix
⤴ Laser ⤵		Ink Jet
⤵ Ink Jet ⤴		Laser
Thermal		Thermal

Exercise 10B

10.4 Key in the following text, using a justified right margin and double spacing for the first paragraph only:

SHATTERING THE PEACE (CAPS and centre)

Aircraft, alarms, traffic, neighbours – noise is a serious matter. It can cause excessive nuisance and great distress. The effects are impossible to assess because what irritates one person slightly can drive another person to distraction and damage their health.

It all depends on the length of time, the amount and the type of noise, as well as on the individual's personality and character. Whilst most people are prepared to tolerate noise wh. has a recognisable purpose and a limited time span, such as a car alarm or road works, a noise problem wh. continues for a very long time, disturbing life to a great extent, can cause extreme reactions. Regulations and bye-laws exist to control the incidence of noise and complaints shd. be made to the nearest Environmental Health Office.

Complaints usually fall into the following categories:

Noisy neighbours
Building sites and road works
Pubs, clubs and restaurants
Burglar alarms and car alarms
Aircraft and traffic noise.

10.5 Proof-read your work carefully, using the spelling tool.

10.6 Save and print your document using filename **EX10B**. Check your print-out with that at the back of the book. If you find any errors, correct them.

10.7 Exit the program if you have finished working or continue straight on to the next unit.

UNIT 11 *Personal business letters*

At the end of Unit 11 you will have learnt how to
- *complete a personal business letter*
- *insert a new page break*
- *complete an envelope*

Keying in a personal business letter (using 'blocked' style with open punctuation)

- Type your own address (or sender's address) at top left-hand side of the letter.
- Block everything at the left-hand margin (date, addressee, salutation, subject heading, all paragraphs and complimentary close) – do not indent paragraphs or centre items.
- Always remember to date the letter with today's date at the left margin – it is also acceptable to position the date flush with the right margin.
- Use open punctuation – no punctuation above or below the body of the letter (i.e. date, addressee, salutation or complimentary close).
- Leave at least one clear line space between the different parts of the letter – date, addresses, salutation, etc.
- Leave at least one clear line space between paragraphs.
- If the salutation is formal, e.g. 'Dear Sir or Madam', finish your letter with complimentary close: 'Yours faithfully'.
- If the salutation is informal, e.g. 'Dear Mrs Smith', finish your letter with the complimentary close: 'Yours sincerely'.
- Leave several clear lines for the person sending the letter to write his or her signature.

Exercise 11A

11.1 Key in Exercise 11A - follow the layout of the letter as shown but allow wordwrap to make the line endings. There is no need for you to type the instructions shown in small italic print in the margin – they are simply a guide to help you identify the different parts of a letter.

11.2 Save your document using filename **EX11A**.

Exercise 11A

Secretarial Department   *address of sender*
Maynesbury Secretarial College
Netherley Road
MAYNESBURY
MY1 4BR

Leave one clear line

Today's date   *date in full*

Leave one clear line

Mr/Miss Student   *name and address of addressee*
77 Anywhere Avenue
SOMETOWN
ST3 2MN

Leave one clear line

Dear Mr/Miss Student   *salutation*

Leave one clear line

This is an example of a personal letter. There is no   *body of letter*
punctuation in the addresses or the date, and no
comma after the salutation. Punctuation is used only
in the body of the letter when it is necessary. In
the fully blocked style, every line begins at the
left margin.

Leave one clear line

You will normally use single line spacing for the
paragraphs and leave one clear line space between
paragraphs. Study the layout of this letter and set
your own letter out in this way.

Leave one clear line

Yours sincerely   *complimentary close*

Leave five clear lines

                                                                      space for signature

P D Walker (Mrs)   *name of signatory (sender)*

Envelopes

You may be required to produce an envelope to go with your letter. In some examinations it may be acceptable to produce the envelope on a typewriter. You may, however, use Word for Windows to create and print envelopes direct. You should check with your printer manual first to see if your printer is capable of printing envelopes, or if it needs any special settings.

Envelope layout

- Begin approximately *one-third* across and *half-way* down the envelope
- Key in each part of the address on a separate line
- Key in the town in CAPITALS
- Key in the postcode on a separate line leaving one space between the two parts of the postcode

```
                                    Mr/Miss Student
                                    77 Anywhere Avenue
                                    SOMETOWN
                                    ST3 2MN
```

Envelopes

- You can automatically insert the delivery address for the envelope from the corresponding letter by highlighting the delivery address at the top of your letter
- If you wish, you can also enter an address for the letter to be returned – this will be displayed at the top left-hand corner of the envelope. *This is not normally required for examination purposes*
- Select: <u>T</u>ools, <u>E</u>nvelopes and Labels

The **Envelopes and Labels** dialogue box is displayed on screen:

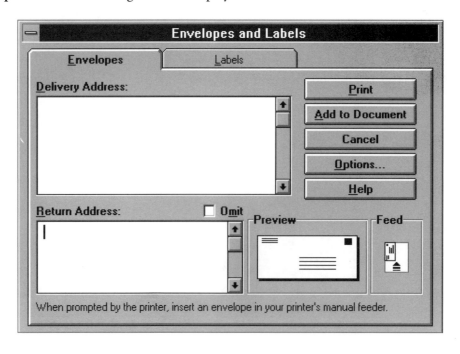

- Select the **Envelopes** tab
- In the **Delivery Address** box either:
  1. Accept the proposed delivery address *or*
  2. Type the address you wish to send the letter to

- In the **Return Address** box either:
  1. Accept the proposed return address *or*
  2. Type the address you wish the letter to be returned to *or*
  3. Select: **Omit** check box if you don't want a return address

- Select the **Options** button: Select: **Envelopes Options** to choose envelope size, font style

  Select: **Printing Options** to choose type of feed, etc. (Word will recommend the feed method but you may over-ride this and select a different feed method if necessary)

  Select: **OK**

- To *print* the envelope: Insert the envelope as shown in the feed box and then select the **Print** button

11.3 Produce an envelope for the letter completed in Exercise 11A following the guidelines given.

11.4 Unless it is already on your screen, open the document EX11A.

11.5 Position the cursor at the end of the document. Insert a new page break.

 Insert a new page break

When keying in a long document, Word automatically inserts page breaks for you. These are called *soft* page breaks. You can choose to insert a page break yourself whenever you want to start a new page – e.g. the start of a new chapter. This is called a *manual* or *hard* page break.

Keyboard	**Mouse and menu**
Position cursor where you want to insert the page break:	
Press: **Ctrl + ↵** (Return)	Select: **Insert**, **Break**, **Page Break**, OK

Exercise 11B

11.6 Key in the following document from the manuscript draft:

---

27 Bridge Road
Moorley Park
SELLERSBY
SL3 RB1

Mr D Tillotson
27 Marsh Lane
SELLERSBY
SL2 ER4

Dear David

May I take this opp. to thank you once again for the excellent luncheon wh. my wife and I enjoyed at your house last Sun. It was much more relaxing to be able to discuss bus. in such pleasant surroundings, away from the pressures of the office demands. I feel confident that we will def. be able to expand on our marketing plans. I sh. recom. to the Marketing Team that we commence a re-draft of our standard co. advert. in line w. the modifications we discussed. Please convey my sincere thanks to your wife for her hospitality.

Yours sncly.

George Frazer

11.7 Save and print your document using filename **EX11B**. Check your print-outs with the printed exercise in this unit and with those at the back of the book. If you find any errors, make the necessary corrections. Keep your print-out of the first letter (EX11A) for future reference on correct letter layout.

11.8 Produce an envelope to go with the letter in Exercise 11B.

11.9 Exit the program if you have finished working or continue straight on to the next unit.

UNIT 12 Consolidation 2

Task 12A Key in the following document using a ragged right margin. Remember to enter today's date. Save and print a copy of your file – using the filename **TASK12A**.

---

13 Benington Ave.
LEEDS
LS3 4PR

Mrs K Begum
Hotel Attoria
23 Latterley Cres.
SHEFFIELD
SH3 9TR

Dr. Mrs Begum

In response to yr. recent advert., I would like to request further information about the special accom. rates available during August at yr. hotel.

My wife & I would like to take a long week-end break from Fri. - Mon. in the third week of Aug.

We sh. require a twin-bedded room with adjoining en suite facilities. I would appreciate it if you could recom. any interesting evening entertainment wh. is taking place in the area at the time of our stay.

I will forward the necy. deposit to secure the booking as soon as I have recd. the relevant details along w. the names of any reputable local restaurants from you.

Yours scly.

M Norton (Mr)

Task 12B Produce an envelope to go with the letter in TASK12A.

Task 12C

Key in the following document using single-line spacing and a justified right margin. Make amendments as shown and correct the circled words. Save and print a copy of your file – use filename **TASK12C**.

Safety on the Road [centre + underline]

Car manufacturers now take safety even more seriously. Safety features sell cars. Perhaps in the past, buyers wanted speed, glamour and status but they are now more conscious of safety. A range of key features: Adverts offer a

- Airbags
- Side-impact bars
- Anti-lock brakes
- Seat belt grabbers and tensioners
- Rear seatbelts (three-point)
- Integrated children's seats

EC tests are currently being revised, particularly with ref. to side and offset impacts. Car designers are anticipating recommendations and competing for buyers on the safety issue. The Department of Transport has published a list of the safest cars but models less than 3 years old are not yet included.

Task 12D

Retrieve the document TASK12C (unless it is already on your screen). Amend as follows:

- Insert the following text so that it becomes the fourth paragraph – for this paragraph only, use double-line spacing and inset by 1 inch at left and right margins

---

Designers are definitely working hard to improve the modern car and improvements are continually being made but safety is now very much a marketing feature and the buyer is left to assess which features are really effective

---

- Search for the word **designers** and replace throughout with **manufacturers**
- Change the heading to capitals and copy to the end of the document (retain the centred display)
- Change the right margin to ragged

Save and print a copy of your file – use filename **TASK12D**.

UNIT 13 Examination practice 2

This examination practice unit is for RSA Core Text Processing Skills.

Task 13A Key in the following document. Save and print a copy of your file – use filename **TASK13A**.

> 27 Sunnybank Ave.
> HARROGATE
> HR5 2SP
>
> R Melling & Son Ltd
> 32 Richmond Rd.
> NOTTINGHAM
> NG7 8WR
>
> Dr. Sirs
>
> I have recently recd. copies of your cat. and price list for dried flower arrangements & silk plants. Unfortunately, I bel. the prices quoted may no longer be accurate as the copies were passed to me thro' a friend some considerable time ago.
>
> I would, therefore, appreciate it if you could send me an up-to-date price list and cat. for wh. I enclose a large stamped addressed envelope.
>
> There is a ref. in your old brochure to samples of raffia, cane & basketware which you also supply and I would be very interested in receiving more details on these.
>
> I look forward to hearing from you shortly.
>
> Yrs. ffly.
>
> L De Sousa (Miss)

Task 13B Produce an envelope to go with the letter in **TASK13A**.

Task 13C Key in the following document using single-line spacing and a justified right margin. Make amendments as shown and correct the circled words. Save and print a copy of your file – use filename **TASK13C**.

COMMUNICATING WITH WORDS

It could be said that the first IT revolution took place over 500 yrs. ago when printing w. movable type was invented by Johannes Gutenberg. The armies of scribes and manuscript makers (the early word processing operators?) gave way to the production of books by mechanical means although the printing types imitated hand-written work. It is ironic that, in the midst of another revolution – IT, calligraphy is making a come-back. The practice of calligraphy, wh. means 'beautiful handwriting' was first revived during the Arts & Crafts movement at the end of last century.

Task 13D Retrieve the document TASK13C (unless it is already on your screen). Amend as follows:

- Insert the following text so that it becomes the second paragraph – for this paragraph only, use double-line spacing and inset by 1 inch at left and right margins

Calligraphy allows a unique, personalised and creative document, and the grace & beauty of the letterforms make such an item rather special. Mass communications are obviously best transmitted by the wonders of IT, but

- Search for the word **IT** and replace throughout with **information technology**
- Underline the heading and copy to the end of the document (retain the centred display)
- Change the right margin to ragged

Save and print a copy of your file – use filename **TASK13D**.

UNIT 14 — Tabulation

At the end of Unit 14 you will have learnt how to
- *set a new tab*
- *delete an individual tab*
- *change the position of a tab setting*
- *delete all tab settings together*
- *reset tabs at regular intervals*

Tabulation

Data is often presented in columns within letters, memos and reports to convey information quickly and clearly. Tabulated columns of information are also used for separate tables and accounts.

If you align text on screen by pressing the Spacebar, rather than using tabstops, it may not line up when you print, so it is more accurate to set tab stops at appropriate points on the ruler line. On some keyboards the tab key is labelled **Tab** and on others shown as |⇆|.

In Word for Windows the tab settings are normally defaulted (i.e. previously set) to every 0.5 inch. Each time you press the tab key you indent the line by 0.5 inch. You can often complete a table satisfactorily using the default tabs. There will be times, however, especially if you are typing a table with columns containing a lot of data or where space is limited, when you will need to *set, delete* or *change* the position of the default tab settings.

When keying in a table:

- Use capitals or underlining to emphasize the column headings and leave a clear line space between the heading and the information below.
- Leave sufficient space between the headings to allow for the longest line of each column.
- Set a tab stop for the longest line in each column, in the appropriate places, remembering to include at least three blank spaces between columns. It looks better if you leave equal amounts of space between columns but this is not absolutely necessary. If you decide to use default tabs the spaces will probably be unequal.
- Key in the columns in double or single-line spacing according to the instructions provided or amount of space available on the page.
- Depending on the type of display, you can choose a *left-aligned tab* (to block entries to the left), or a *right-aligned tab* (to block entries to the right), or a *decimal tab* (to wrap decimal numbers

around the decimal point), or a *centred tab* (to centre each entry around the tab stop). You can set a combination of different types of tab stops within the document and even on the same line if appropriate. For example:

476	476	476.20	476
12463	12463	12463.98	12463
5	5	5.00	5
↑	↑	↑	↑
Left-aligned tab	Right-aligned tab	Decimal tab	Centred tab

- You should leave at least one clear line after the tabulation work before continuing with any further portions of text.
- To add, delete or change tab stops in Word, you should first select all the paragraphs in which you want to edit the settings. Then, make your tab-stop changes.

Tabulation

Mouse and ruler method

- First: Select all the paragraphs in which you want to add, delete or move tab stops:

Add a tab	Click on the **Tab Alignment** button at far left of horizontal ruler until the type of tab alignment you want is displayed:
	Left-aligned tab Decimal tab
	Right-aligned tab Centred tab
	Click the mouse pointer on the horizontal ruler at the place where you want to set the tab stop
Delete a tab	Click and drag the tab marker off the horizontal ruler; release the mouse button
Move a tab	Drag the tab marker to the right or left on the horizontal ruler
Change type of tab alignment	Drag the tab marker off the horizontal ruler Follow instructions for 'add a tab'

Mouse and menu method

- First: Select all the paragraphs in which you want to add, delete or move tab stops
- Select: **F̲ormat**, **T̲abs**. The **Tabs** dialogue box is displayed on screen

Add a tab *(complete for each tab)*	Key in required position in the **T̲ab Stop Position** box (e.g. 1.5 inches) Select type of tab alignment from the **Alignment** box options (e.g. L̲eft) Click on **S̲et**. Click on **OK**
Delete a tab	Select the tab to be deleted from the **T̲ab Stop Position** box Click on **Cle̲ar**
Delete all tabs	Click on **Clear A̲ll**
Move a tab	Follow instructions for 'delete a tab' then 'add a tab' in new position
Change type of tab alignment	Highlight the tab to be changed in the **T̲ab Stop Position** box Select the new type of tab alignment from the **Alignment** box options Click on **S̲et**
Reset default tab stops	Select or key in the distance you want between tab stops in the **De̲fault Tab Stops** box (e.g. 0.5 inch); click on **OK**

Exercise 14A

14.1 Set tabs to every 0.5 inch if these are not already set by the program default (check the **Format**, **Tabs** dialogue box). Key in the following text. After typing the bracketed letter at the beginning of each line, press the tab key once to reach the first set tab stop.

HOLIDAY FRANCE

The following details will be required by the end of next month in order to plan ahead for the French trip:

A)   Number of students who intend to go on the trip.
B)   The most suitable method of receiving payments.
C)   An agreed date for the first information evening.
D)   Closing date for entries.

14.2 Press: ↵ several times to leave a gap before the next exercise.

Exercise 14B

14.3 Key in the following exercise (using the default tab settings, press the tab key to enter the days of the week in the correct positions and before each numerical entry of the table):

FRENCH COURSE ATTENDANCE MONDAY-FRIDAY

Week beginning 2 December

	Mon	Tue	Wed	Thu	Fri
FRENCH BEGINNERS:	26	22	25	17	15
FRENCH GCSE:	18	16	19	18	17
FRENCH A-LEVEL	16	12	13	19	14

You may retain the abbreviations for the days of the week

14.4 Press: ↵ several times to leave a gap before the next exercise.

Exercise 14C

14.5 Delete all existing tabs. Then set left-aligned tab stops at **1.75 inches** and **3.5 inches** only.

14.6 Check that you have set the tab stops in the correct position by pressing the tab key twice. The cursor should move across the screen to position **1.75 inches** and then **3.5 inches** on your ruler line.

14.7 Key in the following exercise:

HOLIDAY ROTA

MEMBER OF STAFF	DATES	NO OF DAYS
Mr Ridgeway	July 9 - July 16	7
Mrs Gaukroger	July 17 - July 21	14
Mrs Lightowler	August 2 - August 9	7
Mr Simms	August 10 - August 31	21

14.8 Press: ↵ several times to leave a gap before the next exercise.

Exercise 14D

14.9 Set tab stops in the appropriate places. Key in the following exercise:

STATIONERY STOCK

<u>Quantity</u>	<u>Description</u>	<u>Price each (£)</u>
36	Blue ball point pens	0.75
24	A4 line pads	1.25
9	Shorthand pads	0.60
48	Erasers	0.20

14.10 Press: ↵ several times to leave a gap before the next exercise.

Exercise 14E

14.11 Set the tab stops as appropriate for the column entries below (i.e. column a = left-aligned, column b = centred, column c = right-aligned, column d = decimal). Then key in the exercise.

Chair	Wicker	56	24.00
Settee	Tapestry	8	135.50
Stool	Pine	147	9.50

14.12 Save and print your document (Exercises 14A –14E) using filename **EX14**. Check your print-out with the exercises shown in this unit. If you find any errors, retrieve the document and correct.

14.13 Reset left-aligned tab stops to every 0.5 inch.

14.14 Exit the program if you have finished working or continue straight on to the next unit.

UNIT 15 Memorandums and abbreviations

At the end of Unit 15 you will have learnt how to
- *complete a memorandum*
- *recognize and expand abbreviations*

Memorandums

A memorandum is a document sent 'internally' to convey information to people who work in the same organization. At the top of the document it is customary to enter whom the document is being sent *from*, whom it is being sent *to*, and to include a *reference*, the *date* of sending and usually a *subject heading*. There is no complimentary close.

Many organizations prefer the items on the memo to be set out and aligned as shown in the example. Some people like to sign their memos but this is not absolutely necessary.

MEMORANDUM

From: Sender **Ref:** AZ456

To: Receiver **Date:** today's

SUBJECT HEADING

Study the layout and spacing of the top part of the memo carefully.

Type the body of the memo in single-line spacing with a clear line space between paragraphs.

Abbreviations

accom.	accommodation	exp.	experience
a/c(s).	account(s)	gov(s)	government(s)
ack.	acknowledge	gntee(s).	guarantee(s)
advert(s).	advertisement(s)	immed.	immediately
appt(s).	appointment(s)	incon.	inconvenient/ence
approx.	approximately	mfr(s).	manufacturer(s)
bel.	believe	misc.	miscellaneous
bus.	business	necy.	necessary
cat(s).	catalogue(s)	opp(s).	opportunity/ies
cttee(s).	committee(s)	rec(s).	receipt(s)
co(s).	company/ies	rec.	receive
def.	definitely	recd.	received
dev.	develop	recom.	recommend
dr.	dear	ref(s).	reference(s)
ex.	exercise	refd.	referred
exp(s).	expense(s)	resp.	responsible

sec(s).	secretary/ies	thro'	through
sep.	separate	wh.	which
sh.	shall	wd.	would
shd.	should	w.	with
sig(s).	signature(s)	wl.	will
suff.	sufficient	yr(s).	year(s)
temp.	temporary	yr(s).	your(s)

Days of the week, e.g.:
Mon. Monday
Tues. Tuesday

Months of the year, e.g.:
Jan. January
Feb. February

Words in addresses, e.g.:
Cres. Crescent
Dr. Drive

Complimentary close, e.g.:
ffly. faithfully
scly. sincerely

Note: You should retain other commonly used abbreviations such as **etc.**, **e.g.**, **NB**, **Ltd**. You can retain the & sign in company names but you should never use the & sign in text.

Exercise 15A

15.1 Key in the following memorandum, expanding all the abbreviations as you go along and making any other amendments indicated. Check that you have keyed in the correct abbreviations from the list in this unit.

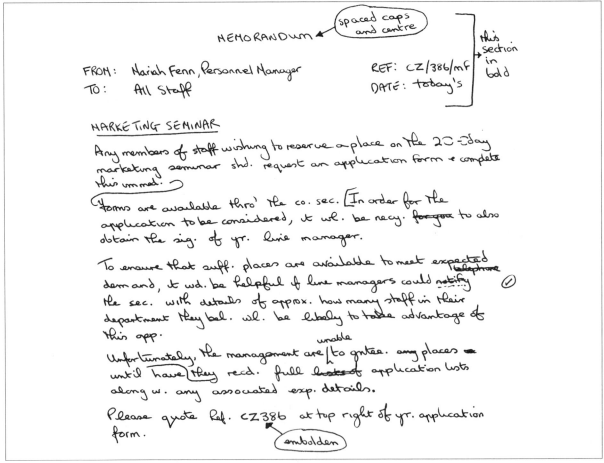

15.2 Save and print your document using filename **EX15A**. Check your printout with that at the back of the book. If you find any errors, retrieve the document and correct.

15.3 Exit the program if you have finished working or continue straight on to the next unit.

UNIT 16 *Indent text, change line length, enumerated paragraphs*

At the end of Unit 16 you will have learnt how to
- *indent blocks of text or paragraphs*
- *change the line length for the whole document*
- *set out enumerated paragraphs*

 Indent – 'wrap around' or temporary indent feature

In Unit 3 you practised changing the left and right margins to inset the text to a different line length. Another method of indenting blocks of text, or paragraphs, is to use the indent function which is available on Word.

You should not confuse paragraph indentation with margins. 'Indenting' moves the text in or out from the margins. The margins set the overall width of the main text and the amount of space between the main text and the edges of the page. If you are asked to leave a specified amount of horizontal space at any point in a task, you may choose to use either the indent function or alter the margin settings as appropriate.

When you operate the indent feature, the insertion pointer moves to the first preset tab stop (usually defaulted to 0.5 inch from the left margin). As you carry on keying in, the text will 'wrap around' the indent point until you operate the command to go back to the original left margin.

In Word, you can choose to indent paragraphs in different ways. You can choose to indent the text from both the left margin and right margin, or from the left margin only. You can also use the indent function for enumerated or bulleted paragraphs – see the information section further on in this unit.

It is often more convenient to use the indent function to indent a single paragraph rather than changing the margins.

> This is an example of a paragraph with a first-line indent.
>
> This is an example of a paragraph indented at both left and right margins.
>
> This is an example of a paragraph with a hanging indent.
>
> a) This is an example of an indented and enumerated paragraph.

To indent a paragraph

Using the keyboard:

Indent to the next tab stop	Press: **Ctrl + M**
Indent to the previous tab stop	Press: **Ctrl + Shift +M**
Indent as a hanging paragraph	Press: **Ctrl + T**
Remove indent and return to standard margins	Press: **Ctrl + Q**

Using the Formatting Toolbar:

Indent to the next tab stop	Click: increase indent
Indent to the previous tab stop	Click: decrease indent

Using the ruler:

Select the paragraph(s) you want to indent

Drag the indent markers to the required position on the horizontal ruler

To set the first-line indent	Drag:
To set the left indent (all lines)	Drag:
To set the first-line and left indents	Drag:
To set the right indent	Drag:

To scroll into the left margin, hold down shift and click the left scroll arrow on horizontal scroll bar. Then drag the indent markers on the horizontal ruler to the required position.

Using the menu:

Select the paragraph(s) you want to indent

From the **Format** menu, select: **Paragraph**, **Indents and Spacing**

Indents and Spacing dialogue box is displayed on screen:

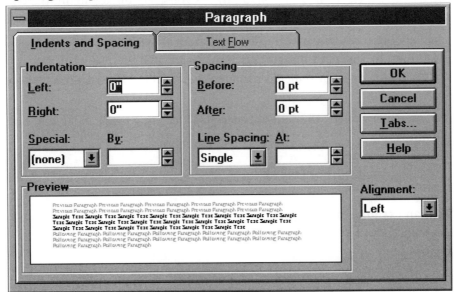

- Select or key in the **Left** and **Right** indent measurements required in the **Indentation** boxes
- Select **First Line** or **Hanging** indents from the list in the **Special** drop-down box
- Select an alternative measurement for the first line or hanging indent from the **By** drop-down box if the default one is not appropriate
- You can change the paragraph alignment from the **Alignment** drop-down box if you wish
- Click on **OK**

Changing the typing line length

You may be asked to change the 'typing line length' (or typing line) of a document to a fixed number of characters. This is achieved by either *indenting*, using the indent function, or *insetting the margins*. (It is not always possible in word processing to be completely accurate in this respect and examiners should be aware of this and be lenient in their marking of this feature.)

Refer back to Unit 3 for instructions on changing margins. Use the mouse/ruler method so that you can see the margin markers move on screen. Use the ruler and the default tabs (every $1/2$ inch) as a guide (e.g. to set a line length of 5 inches, you could position the left margin marker at 1 inch on the ruler and the right margin marker at 6 inches on the ruler).

Using this method, you can change margins:

- before keying in
- after keying in
- for a section of text only

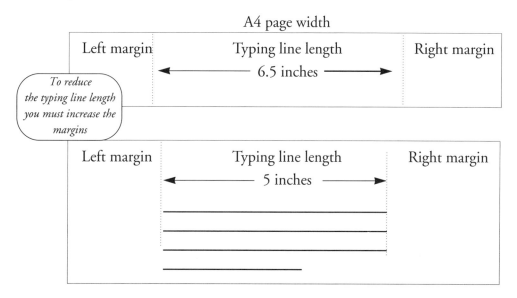

 Exercise 16A

16.1 Retrieve the file you saved from Unit 5: EX5D.

16.2 Change the typing line length of the document to 4½ inches.

16.3 Using the indent function, indent the second, third and fourth paragraphs by 0.5 inch at the left margin only.

16.4 Save and print your document using filename **EX16A**. Check your print-out with that at the back of the book. If you find your layout does not match, reread the information and amend.

 Exercise 16B

16.5 Retrieve the file you saved from Unit 15: EX15A.

16.6 Change the typing line length of the document to 5 inches.

16.7 Using the indent function

- indent the second, third and fourth paragraphs by 1 inch at left and right margins
- indent the last paragraph by 0.5 inch at left margin

16.8 Save and print your document using filename **EX16B**. Check your print-out with that at the back of the book. If you find your layout does not match, reread the information and amend.

 ## Enumerated paragraphs

Word can quickly create enumerated or bulleted paragraphs. Enumeration shows sequence while bullets emphasize separate items in a list. You can choose different styles of enumeration – capital letters, lower-case letters, numbers or roman numerals, any of which can be followed by a bracket or a full stop or nothing. If you add, delete or reorder enumerated items, Word will automatically update the sequence for you. You will usually leave one clear line space between enumerated items.

Example of a bulleted list:
- apples
- oranges
- pears

Example of enumerated paragraphs:
A) Fred likes apples but he doesn't like pears.

B) Susan likes pears and apples.

Enumerated or bulleted paragraphs

Keyboard

- Position cursor at the beginning of the paragraph to begin with an enumeration:
- Type: The enumeration, e.g. A)
- Press: **Tab** key (to set the indent for the first line)
- Press: **Ctrl + T** (to set the 'hanging' indent for all subsequent lines of the paragraph)

Mouse and toolbar

- Position cursor at the beginning of the paragraph(s) to begin with an enumeration or bullet:

- Click: ▤ bullet button *or* ▤ numbering button on the **Formatting** Tool Bar

Note: You can change the numbering style (from letters, numbers or roman numerals) through the **Format, Bullets and Numbering** menu – see below. The style you select from the menu is adopted by the numbering or bullets button on the Formatting Tool Bar until you change it again.

Mouse and menu

- Position cursor at the beginning of the paragraph(s) to begin with an enumeration or bullet:
- Select: **Format, Bullets and Numbering** from the menu
- Select: **Bullets** or **Numbering**
- Click: On the style you require (a blue outline appears on the selected box)
- Click: **OK**

Optional facilities:

- Click: The **H̲anging Indent** box to toggle the **x** on or off to determine whether or not you want the paragraph lines to wrap around the indent point (check the preview box display)
- Click: **M̲odify** if you need to make any more changes to the enumeration style
- Click: **R̲emove** to remove an enumeration or bullet

End enumeration or bullets

When you press ↵ to start a new paragraph, Word carries over the enumeration or bullet style (list formatting) to the next paragraph until you 'interrupt' the list.

*To **interrupt** a list:*

- Position pointer on the line below the last item you want to 'interrupt' the list or stop enumeration:
- Click: Right mouse button and select: **Stop Numbering**

  or

- Click: Bullet or numbering button on the Formatting Tool Bar to 'toggle off'

*To **remove** an enumeration or bullet from one or more items:*

- Select: The item(s) with the enumeration or bullet to be removed
- Click: [≔] bullet button or [≔] numbering button on the **Formatting** Tool Bar

  or

- Select: **R̲emove** from the **F̲ormat, Bullets and N̲umbering** menu

---

Exercise 16C

16.9 Key in the following exercise - remember to leave at least one clear space between enumerated items:

MAYNESBURY MUSEUMS

There are a number of interesting tourist attractions at Maynesbury:

A) MAYNESBURY HALL: Period house and Local History Museum dating in part from the 15th century with 18th century wing designed by Andrew Browning. Displays of costume and pottery and a 'ghost' room.

B) MAYNESBURY MANOR: Small Tudor Manor House built on the site of a Roman fort with exposed Roman wall in grounds. Displays of Roman archaeological material.

C) BRAMSWELL HOUSE: Noted for its collection of pictures, Chippendale furniture and fine porcelain. There is also a bird garden, a lakeside walk and a children's playground.

Please contact the Maynesbury Information Centre, on 0458 389256, for details of:

    a) Reduced entrance rates for parties of 15 or more.

    b) Special discounts for OAPs and the unwaged.

    c) Opening and closing times.

16.10 Save and print your document using filename **EX16C**. Check your print-out with the exercise above. If you find any errors, retrieve the document and correct.

Exercise 16D

16.11 Retrieve the file EX16C unless it is already on your screen.

16.12 Change the line length for the whole document to 5¼ inches.

16.13 Change the enumeration style of the paragraphs with capital letters to **numbers**. Indent the same paragraphs by 0.5 inch at left and right margins.

16.14 Change the enumeration style of the paragraphs with lower-case letters to **roman numerals**. Indent the same paragraphs by a further 0.5 inch at left margin only.

16.15 Save and print your document using filename **EX16D**. Check your print-out with that at the back of the book. If you find any errors, retrieve the document and correct.

16.16 Exit the program if you have finished working or continue straight on to the next unit.

UNIT 17 *Allocating vertical space and confirming facts*

At the end of Unit 17 you will have learnt how to
- *leave specified areas of vertical space within a document*
- *confirm facts by checking details from information given previously*

Allocating vertical space

It is often necessary to insert diagrams, photographs or maps on to a page which also contains text. For example, a student record-card may need to have a blank space where the student's photograph could be fixed.

You may be asked to leave space using line spaces, inches, centimetres or millimetres.

Line spaces

When a given number of line spaces is requested, e.g.:

Please leave 6 clear lines here

Press: ↵ the given number of line spaces *plus one* starting from immediately after the last character of the paragraph above the space. For example:

To leave 6 clear lines, press ↵ 7 times

To leave 9 clear lines, press ↵ 10 times

Inches, centimetres, millimetres

When a given measurement is requested, e.g.:

Leave a space 1 inch (25 mm) here for photograph

Please allow space here 5 cm deep (2 inches) for logo

Use Word's paragraph format facility – see instructions 'Allocating vertical space (using paragraph format)'.

Allocating vertical space (using paragraph format)

- Key in all the text for the document before carrying out this procedure
- Delete any clear line spaces *above* the paragraph which is to be placed below the required space, e.g.:

    This is the first paragaph. The requested amount of vertical space is to be allocated after this paragraph.
    This is the second paragraph. The required vertical space is to be inserted before this paragraph. The space between the two paragraphs has been deleted.

- Position the pointer immediately before the first letter of the second paragraph (see above)
- Select: **F**ormat, **P**aragraph from the Menu Bar
- Key in: Required measurement in **Spacing, Before** box (you may use any unit of measurement - e.g. 1 inch or 2 cm or 25 mm)
- Click on **OK**

Note: The above setting will be changed to a point-size measurement and will remain selected until it is changed or deleted.

 ## Confirming facts

When people are writing manuscript copy and wish to save time, they often leave the operator to fill in repeated text such as names, titles, addresses, etc. You will need to check previous correspondence and use your common sense to fill in the missing information.

In elementary examinations, you will not have to 'invent' any missing information, but you will be expected to complete gaps from information given elsewhere in the examination paper. The first letter of each missing word will be given to assist you.

Example

> Dr M A Rashid
> Cotherstone
> 117 Old Main St.
> STANIFORTH
>
> Dear Dr R_____
>
> The proposed work on the renovation of the roof at your home, C_____, is scheduled to...

(The missing words would be Rashid and Cotherstone.)

ALLOCATING VERTICAL SPACE AND CONFIRMING FACTS 77

Exercise 17A

17.1 Starting a new file, key in the following text using single-line spacing and a justified right margin. Press the ↵ key the required number of times to leave space the first time it is requested. Use the paragraph format method to leave space the second time it is requested.

TRAINING PLAN — bold

The aim of our t_____ p_____ is to give all employees the opp. to dev. themselves so that they can contribute effectively to the achievement of the co.'s objectives.

As a mfr. of women's fashion accessories, we bel. that it is necy. to recruit staff who have recd. excellent prior training, whether it be as a designer, a sec. or a machine operator. Although the Personnel Department has been resp. for training in the past, we must now ack. that it is necy. to create a sep. department for staff training. The new Training Department wl. be based at the Castle Ave. site and the following members of staff will be transferred to the ~~Department~~ Section.

leave 9 clear lines here for list of names

Indent by ½" at both sides

An advert. for the following **new** appts. is going to press immed. and the persons appointed shd. be in post by the end of Oct. Temp. posts may be offered in some cases.

leave a space 2" deep here for details of appts.

The first task wl. be to define **overall** training needs within the framework of the bus. plan and taking into account existing staff exp.
An analysis of the knowledge and skills required in the performance of every job may take some time but wl. be a valuable ex. The analysis shd. result in a comprehensive, t_____ p_____ *and ultimately successful*.

17.2 Save and print your work using filename **EX17A**. Check your print-out with that at the back of the book. If you find any errors, correct them and print again if necessary.

Exercise 17B

17.3 Starting a new file, key in the following text, using single-line spacing and an unjustified right margin:

MOVING INTO MANAGEMENT ← centre and underline

Senior management positions in a co. are often filled by external applicants as an injection of new blood, but lower down the organisational scale, existing employees are frequently promoted. [NP] There are two main reasons for the latter policy:

promotion as a reward or spur.
using an existing employee's knowledge of the organisation

Performance appraisal can usually provide suff. evidence of an employee's suitability for further development and the type of management training which would be needed can be easily identified. M_____ training may be ~~made available~~ in several ways: [stet] ~~offered~~

space 2 cm deep to be left here, please

Managers need special characteristics, qualities and relevant previous exp. if they are to be successful. A degree of flexibility and adaptability is required and they shd. be aware of the economic, political and social environment. M_____ t_____ methods can be selected to suit a particular co. or a specific situation:

please leave 12 clear lines here for list

Cos. go to considerable exp. to pay for training and it is therefore vital that a full evaluation is carried out. A pattern of continuous feedback shd. be established to review the success of the programmes.

Without good management, wh. responds both to the needs of the co. and to the individual skills and attributes of the employees*, a bus. is unlikely to succeed.

Please indent last para by 1" at left

17.4 Save and print your work using filename **EX17B**. Check your print-out with that at the back of the book. If you find any errors, correct them and print again if necessary.

UNIT 18 Business letter layout

At the end of Unit 18 you will have learnt how to
- *recognize the difference between a 'personal business letter' and a 'business letter'*
- *complete a business letter*
- *position special marks and enclosure marks*

In Unit 11 you learnt how to produce a personal business letter on plain A4 paper. In elementary examinations, you will be expected to produce a business letter on plain A4 paper.

 Business letter layout

A personal business letter is the type of formal letter you might write at home to an organization or firm referring to matters which are not connected with your work.

A business letter is written on behalf of an organization and is printed or typed on the organization's own letterhead. An attractive letterhead gives a good impression of the organization and contains all relevant details such as telephone and fax numbers. Only the name and address of the addressee (recipient) of the letter have to be typed because the sender's details are already printed on the letterhead.

In elementary examinations, the letter is usually printed on plain A4 paper.

Refer back to Unit 11 to refresh your memory on letter layout.

 Special marks and enclosure marks

Special marks are designed to draw special attention on documents and envelopes to instructions such as:

CONFIDENTIAL, PRIVATE, PERSONAL, URGENT, FOR THE ATTENTION OF…

The special marks should be placed at the top of the document with one clear line space above and below it.

If a letter includes a special mark, this should also be included on the envelope.

Enclosure marks (**Enc** or **Encs**) are used to draw attention to the fact that an item should be included with the main document. This alerts the person preparing the mail to check that the item(s) is actually enclosed, and also the person receiving the correspondence to check that the enclosure(s) has actually been included. If an enclosure is found to be missing, appropriate action can then be taken.

The enclosure mark is usually placed at the end of a letter or memo with one clear line space above and below it.

 ## Automatic date insertion

Word will insert the current date in letters and memorandums.

Date insertion (automatic format)

Keyboard	Mouse/menu
Press: **Alt + Shift + D**	Position pointer in correct place for date to be inserted
	Select: **Insert** from the Menu Bar
	Select: **Date and Time**

The **Date and Time** dialogue box is displayed on screen:

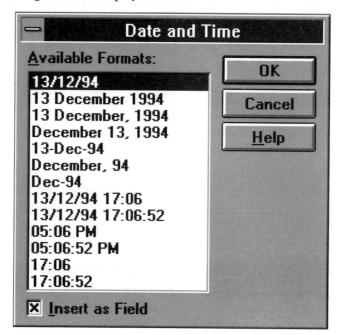

- Word displays a selection of available formats
- In the UK the first style is usually adopted for letters and memos, i.e. **6 August 1994**
- Click to select chosen style
- Check that **Insert as Field** box does not have a tick in it – if so, Word would automatically update the date shown on the document (in some instances, this would be useful)
- Click on **OK**

Exercise 18A

18.1 Starting a new file, key in the following letter, using line spacing as shown. Look back at the letter you completed in Unit 11 to refresh your memory about the parts of a letter.

Our ref: WP/your initials

(today's date)

FOR THE ATTENTION OF LEARNERS

Open Learning Dept
Text Production College
Winword Way
READING   RD4 2WP

Dr Sir or Madam

FULLY-BLOCKED BUSINESS LETTER

Following some work study research about 30 yrs ago, it was decided that bus. letters could be more quickly prepared if the fully-blocked style were adopted.

At the same time, open punctuation was also introduced. Typists were requested to use commas, full stops etc only in the main body of the letter to make sure that it made sense. Every line begins at the left margin — there is no indentation.

NP W___ P___ examinations have always required a high degree of accuracy.

Yrs ffly.

(leave at least 4 clear lines here for signature)

W P T Utor

18.2 Save your document, using filename **EX18A**.

Exercise 18B

18.3 Open the document EX18A if it is not already on screen. Insert the following information at the appropriate places:

You may be required to include a simple table within your letter. An example is given below:

TOWN OR CITY	COUNTY	COUNTRY
Coventry	Warwickshire	England
Chesterfield	Derbyshire	England
Swansea	West Glamorgan	Wales
Stranraer	Dumfries and Galloway	Scotland

(insert as 3rd para)

All Elementary examinations usually include a bus. letter and you shd. follow the layout you are now learning.

Last para – before Yrs. ffly.

18.4 Save and print your document, using filename **EX18A** (replacing the old file). Check your print-out with that at the back of the book. If you find any errors, correct them.

Keep this letter in an accessible place so that you can refer to it when you produce other letters later.

Exercise 18C

18.5 Starting a new file, key in the following letter:

Our ref   HOMINS/9987334

Dear Sir

HOME AND CONTENTS INSURANCE

Further to your recent telephone call to this office, I have pleasure in giving you details of the types of cover we can offer. I enclose a copy of our HOMEPLUS scheme wh. I hope will be of interest to you.

I hope that this information is suff. for you. As one of the largest insurers in the United Kingdom, we look after the homes of millions of families. We also offer a full range of insurance and investment services and would be pleased to discuss these w. you at any time.

Yours faithfully

T Fryer (Ms)

NORMAN CASTLE PLC

Enc

18.6 Save your file, using filename **EX18C**. Do not print your work at this stage.

Exercise 18D

18.7 Recall the letter saved as EX18C if it is not already on screen. Add the following information to the letter:

Address the letter to: Mrs G H Robins, Sherwood, St John's Cres., NOTTINGHAM, NG6 8PP.
Please change salutation to Dr. Madam and mark letter PRIVATE

3rd paragraph please
(before para – 'I hope that....')

The claim limits are as follows:

BUILDINGS	CONTENTS	VALUABLES	CASH
Set by valuer	£1**2**0,000	£10,000	£500

(The limit for individual items under Contents and Valuables is £1,000)

As I explained to you on **the** telephone, it is better to insure ~~your~~ buildings and contents under one policy so that you can be certain that ~~all~~ everything is covered. The policy will ~~insure~~ **cover** your house, personal belongings and furniture, including money, valuables and the contents of your freezer.

(insert as second paragraph)

18.8 Save and print your document, using filename **EX18C** (replacing the old file). Check your document against the print-out at the back of the book. If you find any errors, correct them and print again if necessary.

18.9 Exit the program if you have finished working or continue straight on to the next unit.

UNIT 19 *Rearranging text*

At the end of Unit 19 you will have learnt how to rearrange text to a specified layout.

Rearranging text in a document

One of the most useful facilities of word processing is the ability to rearrange text on the screen and then print out when all the changes have been made. The first draft is sent to the author of the text who marks up the print-out to show what changes are needed. The word-processor operator can recall the document from disk, process the text and then print out the final copy.

Rearrangement of text is part of elementary text-processing examinations. You have already learnt in previous units how to insert, delete, amend, copy and move portions of text. In this unit you will practise how to combine all these skills within one document.

Exercise 19A

19.1 Starting a new file, key in the following text. Use single-line spacing and a ragged right margin.

COVERING THE WALLS

Wallpaper first came into being as an inexpensive way of making walls more attractive by applying designs. Wallpaper may not seem particularly cheap to us nowadays but home decorating is a job wh. most of us can tackle w. practice.

Special effects can be achieved by the use of different types and shades of paper. A lightweight paper is suitable for bedrooms, while a vinyl-coated paper is a practical choice for kitchens as it can be wiped clean.

Consider the effect you want to achieve and the type of activities likely to take place in the room in question before you begin.

Estimate the number of rolls you will need carefully before you go shopping. Wallcoverings are made in batches and you can only be certain of an exact colour match if the rolls show the same batch number. It is a good idea to buy slightly more than you require and, provided you have not taken the wrapping off, some retailers will accept unused rolls and give a refund or a credit note.

Time spent on preparation is well spent although not the most exciting part of the process. Old wallpaper can be removed by scraping when wet, by chemical strippers or, if particularly stubborn, by steam stripping. If the walls are not as smooth as they shd. be or if the wallpaper to be applied is thin, a lining paper may be needed. This is usually applied in the opposite direction to that of the top paper - horizontally on walls, and parallel with doors and windows on ceilings.

19.2 Save your document, using filename **EX19A**. Do not print your work at this stage.

Exercise 19B

19.3 Open the file EX19A if it is not already on screen. Amend the document as shown below:

COVERING THE WALLS ← *centre and underline*

leave 2 clear lines here

Wallpaper first came into being as an inexpensive way of making walls more attractive ~~by applying designs~~. Wallpaper may not seem particularly cheap to us nowadays but home decorating is a job wh. most of us can tackle w. practice.

leave 2" here for diagram

Special effects can be achieved by ~~the use of~~ different types and ~~shades~~ **colours** of paper. A lightweight paper is suitable for bedrooms, while a vinyl-coated paper is a practical choice for **bathrooms and** kitchens as it can be wiped clean.

~~Consider the effect you want to achieve and the type of activities likely to take place in the room in question before you begin.~~

inset para by ½" at both sides

Estimate the number of rolls you will need carefully <u>before</u> you go shopping. Wallcoverings are made in batches and you can only be certain of an exact colour match if the rolls show the same batch number. It is a good idea to buy slightly more than you require and, provided you have not taken the **cellophane** wrapping off, some retailers will accept **return of** unused rolls and give a refund or a credit note.

✓ Time spent on preparation is well spent although not the most exciting part of the process. Old wallpaper can be removed by scraping when wet, by ~~chemical~~ strippers or, if particularly stubborn, by steam stripping. If the walls are not as smooth as they shd. be or if the wallpaper to be applied is thin, a lining paper may be needed. This is usually applied in the opposite direction to ~~that of~~ the top paper - horizontally on walls, and parallel with/doors and windows on ceilings. **main**

Take care when using scaffolding or ladders. Make sure they are stable and don't let children play on them.

When working around light fittings and plugs switch covers, always switch off electricity at the mains.

19.4 Save and print a copy of your document, using filename **EX19A** (replacing the old file). Check your document against the print-out at the back of the book. If you find any errors, correct them and print again if necessary.

Exercise 19C

19.5 Open the file EX19A if it is not already on screen. Move the paragraphs as shown below. Refer back to Unit 2 to refresh your memory on how to do this.

<u>COVERING THE WALLS</u> ← remove underline

Wallpaper first came into being as an inexpensive way of making walls more attractive. Wallpaper may not seem particularly cheap to us nowadays but home decorating is a job which most of us can tackle with practice.

— retain at least 2" here

Special effects can be achieved by different types and colours of paper. A lightweight paper is suitable for bedrooms, while a vinyl-coated paper is a practical choice for bathrooms and kitchens as it can be wiped clean.

> Estimate the number of rolls you will need carefully <u>before</u> you go shopping. Wallcoverings are made in batches and you can only be certain of an exact colour match if the rolls show the same batch number. It is a good idea to buy slightly more than you require and, provided you have not taken the sellophane wrapping off, some retailers will accept return of unused rolls and give a refund or a credit note.

remove indents on this paragraph

Time spent on preparation is well spent although not the most exciting part of the process. Old wallpaper can be removed by scraping when wet, by chemical strippers or, if particularly stubborn, by steam stripping. If the walls are not as smooth as they should be or if the wallpaper to be applied is thin, a lining paper may be needed. This is usually applied in the opposite direction to the top paper - horizontally on walls, and parallel with main doors and windows on ceilings.

Take care when using ladders or scaffolding. Make sure they are stable and don't let children play on them. When working around light fittings and switch covers, always switch off electricity at the mains.

19.6 Save and print a copy of your document, using filename **EX19A** (replacing the old file). Check your document against the print-out at the back of the book. If you find any errors, correct them and print again if necessary.

Exercise 19D

19.7 Starting a new file, key in the following text. Use single-line spacing and a justified right margin.

THE YORKSHIRE AND HUMBERSIDE REGION

This famous region of England covers a very large area stretching from Spurn Point on the East coast to the picturesque village of Clapham in the Pennines. Its northern boundary reaches Teeside while the southern border, south of Sheffield, borders Derbyshire.

North Yorkshire is the largest of the four areas within the region with Humberside as second largest. The areas of West Yorkshire and South Yorkshire, although smaller in terms of square miles, are much more densely populated.

The attractions of Humberside include 80 kilometres of safe, sandy beaches. Maritime heritage centres and traditional seaside towns prevail on the coast while inland are attractive market towns and historic halls. The longest single span suspension bridge in the world - the Humber Bridge - is a sight worth seeing.

The landscape of North Yorkshire is more dramatic with large expanses of wild moors, steep-sided valleys and a host of medieval castles and abbeys. The coastline too is striking with its high cliffs and sweeping bays, providing lovely settings for the resorts of Scarborough and Whitby.

South Yorkshire was said to be the crucible of the industrial revolution - the heart of the coal and steel industries. Industrial heritage is a particular feature of the cities and towns yet a short drive will bring you to spectacular, open countryside.

19.8 Save your document, using filename **EX19D**. Do not print your work at this stage.

19.9 Recall this document (EX19D) and amend as shown.
Save under same filename and print one copy.

Indent first para by 1" at left

embolden heading please

THE YORKSHIRE AND HUMBERSIDE REGION

leave 1.5 cm clear

This famous region of England covers a ~~very~~ large area stretching from Spurn Point on the East coast to the picturesque village of Clapham in the Pennines. Its northern boundary ~~reaches~~ *stretches to* Teesside while the southern border, south of Sheffield, borders Derbyshire.

North Yorkshire is the largest of the four areas within the region with Humberside as second largest. The areas of West Yorkshire and South Yorkshire, although smaller in terms of square miles, are much more densely populated.

The attractions of Humberside include *approx.* 80 kilometres of safe, sandy beaches. Maritime heritage centres and traditional seaside towns prevail on the coast while inland are attractive market towns and historic halls. The longest single span suspension bridge in the world - the Humber Bridge - is a sight worth seeing. *(del.)*

The landscape of North Yorkshire is more dramatic with large expanses of wild moors, steep-sided valleys and a host of medieval castles and abbeys. The coastline ~~too~~ is striking with its high cliffs and sweeping bays, providing lovely settings for the resorts of Scarborough and Whitby.

South Yorkshire was said to be the crucible of the industrial revolution - the heart of the coal and steel industries. Industrial heritage is a particular feature of the cities and towns yet a short drive will bring you to spectacular, open countryside.

✓ *Industrial museums exist ~~abound~~ also in W__ Y__, w. emphasis on the textile industry. The cities of Leeds, Bradford and Halifax demonstrate the prosperity of the area in the 19th century thro' the magnificent municipal buildings.*

There are lots of other museums to interest the visitor, ranging from the Bronte Parsonage at Haworth to the National Museum of Photography, Film and Television in Bradford.

UNIT 20 Consolidation 3

Task 20A Retrieve the letter stored under filename TASK12A. Delete the first address – 13 Benington Avenue… Insert the following information where indicated. Save and print a copy of your file – use filename **TASK20A**.

Please insert immediately after Yours sincerely:
MERIDIAN MARKETING SERVICES

Mark the letter: URGENT

Delete the 2nd paragraph and replace with:

My co. is interested in booking approx. 4 sep. bus. conferences during Aug. for wh. we would require suff. overnight accom. for delegates attending the conference as well as hiring the conference suite itself.

Add the following text and table as the 3rd paragraph:

Details of our requirements are as follows:

CONFERENCE DATES	DELEGATES	SPECIAL REQUIREMENTS
Aug. 2 - Aug. 4	12	3 Vegetarian
Aug. 7 - Aug. 10	10	1 Wheelchair access
Aug. 13 - Aug. 15	8	None
Aug. 26 - Aug. 28	16	4 Vegetarian

Task 20B

Key in the text below. Use a justified right margin. Save and print a copy of your file – use filename **TASK20B**.

MEMORANDUM ← centre & spaced caps

(this section in bold)

FROM: Val Feathers, Headmistress

TO: All Staff

REF: FR/VF

DATE: today's

School Fund-raising for materials ← caps & underline

Please make a note *in your diary* of the following fund-raising events wh. are scheduled to help the school to raise additional money for badly-needed materials. I wd. be grateful if you could support the events wherever possible and offers of assistance are def. welcome. *Volunteers to man the sale are needed urgently.*

(Indent 0.5" at left and right margins)

A) Jumble Sale. The jumble sale will be held in the school hall, Thurs. 27 Oct. at 7.30 pm. Please bring all yr. unwanted jumble, bric-a-brac and misc. items to the school at least 2 days before the sale.

B) Clothes Party. Mrs Versity has kindly volunteered the use of her home for a 'chainstore second's clothes party'. You can called in at any time during the afternoon of Sat. 29 Oct. and try on any of the clothes on display – I am told these will be on sale at vastly reduced prices from those in the normal high street shops & cats. Mrs V—— will donate the 10% commission on all goods sold towards the purchase of new school materials.

C) Trivia Quiz Night. Following the last successfull 'T—— Q—— N——' we sh. now hold a second event. The evening will be held at the Wayfarers Inn. We urgently need 4 teams. Please contact Mr Halstead at all possible for you to be a team players.

If you have any other suggestions for fund-raising events, please let me have details as soon as possible.

(double-line spacing for this paragraph)

We are in great need of 2 new computers, in addition to other materials needed for the new library.

Task 20C

Retrieve the document stored under filename TASK20B. Amend where shown. Save and print a copy of your file – use filename **TASK20C**.

MEMORANDUM

FROM: Val Feathers, Headmistress   REF: FR/VF

TO: All Staff   DATE: today's

SCHOOL FUND-RAISING FOR MATERIALS

Please make a note ~~in your diary~~ of the following fund-raising events which are scheduled to help the school to raise additional money for badly-needed materials.

I would be grateful if you could support the events wherever possible and offers of assistance are ~~definitely~~ **especially** welcome.

A) Jumble Sale. The jumble sale will be held in the School Hall [u.c.], Thursday 27 October at 7.30 pm. Please bring all your unwanted jumble, bric-a-brac and miscellaneous items to the School Office [u.c.] at least 2 days before the sale. Volunteers to man the sale are needed urgently.

C) Clothes Party. Mrs Versity has kindly volunteered the use of her home for a 'chainstore seconds clothes party'. You can call in at any time during the afternoon of Saturday, 29 October and try on any of the clothes on display. ~~I am told these will be on sale at vastly reduced prices from those in the normal high street shops and catalogues.~~ Mrs Versity will donate the 10% commission on all goods sold towards the purchase of new school materials.

B) Trivia Quiz Night. Following the last successful 'Trivia Quiz Night', we shall now hold a second event **on Friday, 28 October at 8.30 pm**. The evening will be held at The Wayfarers Inn **who have kindly agreed to let us have a function room free of charge**. We urgently need four teams. Please contact Mr Halstead if it's at all possible for you to be a team player.

If you have any other suggestions for fund-raising events, please let me have details as soon as possible. We are in desperate need of two new computers, in addition to other materials needed for the new library.

D) **Prize Draw. Tickets will be available shortly for the prize draw – more details to follow soon.**

Operator:
* use some form of emphasis for all words underlined
* change right margin to ragged
* remove left and right indent of lettered paragraphs so they become aligned flush with left margin
* find and replace the word 'materials' with 'resources'
* alter line length of document to 5"

UNIT 21 Examination practice 3

This examination practice unit is for RSA, Pitman and City & Guilds Level 1.

Task 21A

Retrieve the letter stored under filename TASK13A. Delete the first address. Mark the letter: **For the attention of the Sales Manager** and insert the following information where indicated. You may use either a justified or ragged margin. Save and print a copy of your file – use filename **TASK21A**.

My co. has recently *completely* modernised (it's) office layout and we wd. like to further enhance the decor with floral arrangements. We wd. be particularly interested to know if you operate a 'hire' service whereby the displays and/or plants can be changed on a regular basis, perhaps ~~weekly~~ *monthly*. I think it might be useful for you to ~~~~ discuss our exact requirements with the different departmental managers concerned – they can be contacted on the following telephone extension numbers:

insert this paragraph so that it becomes 3rd paragraph

DEPARTMENT	MANAGER	EXTENSION
Reception	Susan Evans	2172
Sales	Robert Davies	2110
Marketing	Roman Piatkowski	2134
Secretarial/Administration	Janet Robertshaw	2135

This table to be inserted as telephone extension details of departmental managers

FENWAYS & SMITH LTD

Please insert immediately after: Yours faithfully

Task 21B

Key in the text below. Use a ragged right margin. Save and print a copy of your file – use filename **TASK21B**.

THE COMPACT DISK REVOLUTION

The development of the 5" silver saucer with its tremendous storage capability has opened up a whole new world of multimedia products – business applications, educational programmes, games & electronic ref. books w. video & sound. Audio CDs first appeared when they began to replace vinyl records and cassettes in the 1980s. Mfrs. soon realised the greater potential of this new storage medium & looked towards producing live full-screen video action with CDs replacing videotape.

Full motion video (FMV) is now available at a quality that's claimed to be better than VHS, offering an entire feature film on a couple of disks, lots of music videos on just one, and TV-style video action in computer games.

(Inset 1" at left and right margins)

a) CD-ROM – compact disk read only memory. A disk of 650 Mb can store the equivalent data of a thousand floppy disks.

b) CD-i – c—d— interactive. These work similarly to CD-ROM disks, but being produced to a different standard you can't read a CD-i disk on a PC – you need CD-i hardware.

c) CD-R – recordable c—d— drives. Although these are available, the hardware to enable you to record onto a CD is extremely expensive.

A number of telecom cos. are planning 'video on demand' services. This is where you simply ring up & request a film or TV programme you want to watch to be transmitted down the line to yr. own individual set.

Task 21C Retrieve the document stored under filename TASK 21B. Amend where shown and change to a justified right margin. Find and replace the word **disk** with **disc**. Save and print a copy of your file – use filename **TASK21C**.

THE COMPACT DISK REVOLUTION ← (underline and centre)

← leave 6 clear line spaces here for a photo →

The development of the 5" silver saucer with its tremendous storage ~~capability~~ capacity has opened up a whole new world of multimedia products - business applications, educational programs, games and electronic reference books with sound and video.

~~Audio CDs first appeared when they began to replace vinyl records and cassettes in the 1980s.~~ Manufacturers soon realised the greater potential of this new storage medium and looked towards producing full-screen live video action with CDs replacing videotape.

Full motion video (FMV) is now available at a quality that's claimed to be better than VHS, offering an entire feature film on a couple of disks, lots of music videos on just one, and TV-style video action in computer games.

(change indent to 0.5" at left and right margins)

a) CD-ROM - compact disk read only memory. A disk of 650Mb can store the equivalent data of a thousand floppy disks.

b) CD-i - compact disk interactive. These work ~~similarly~~ in a similar way to CD-ROM disks, but being produced to a different standard you can't read a CD-i disk on a PC - you need CD-i hardware.

c) CD-R - recordable compact disk drives. Although these are available, the hardware to enable you to record onto a CD is extremely expensive.

A number of telecom companies are now planning 'video on demand' services. This is where you simply ring up and request a film or TV programme ~~you want to watch~~ to be transmitted straight down the line to your own individual set.

One of the main problems is that you can only write to a CD once - it can't be 'taped over' so you can't re-use the disk space.

For technical and financial reasons it seems that videotape will still be around in the 21st century as a convenient, practical & economical way of watching TV programmes & films as, unlike the video demand services being planned by cable & telephone cos. it doesn't incur any additional fees.

(add this paragraph to end of document in double line spacing)

(operator: put all the words underlined with ~~~ in BOLD.)

Task 21D

Key in the following document correcting the errors circled and following the amendments. Save and print a copy of your file – use filename **TASK21D**.

M E M O R A N D U M

(spaced caps and centre, bold entire header block)

FROM:	Sandra Jennings	**REF:**	SJ/87
TO:	Lewis Waterhouse	**DATE:**	today's

SNIPPET FOR STAFF EDITORIAL

Here is the small snippet you asked me to write for the staff editorial:

(leave 3 clear line spaces here)

PERFECT PANSIES

Pansies have such a long flowering period and come in so many different hues that they can bring variety to the garden. The ideal site is somewhere where they can have their roots in moist, cool soil and their tops in the sun.

On the other hand, they'd be quite happy to nestle in the dappled shade of larger shrubs.

The compact shape of violas makes them particularly good for edging borders and paths. Both violas and pansies can be grown in containers although it's a pity to restrict the viola's spreading potential.

Print-out checks

Exercise 1A

When you start using Word for Windows, your screen will show the name of the application in the title bar at the top. Immediately below this you will see the menu bar, containing a horizontal list of words, each with the initial letter underlined.

You can select an item in the menu bar by using the mouse or the keyboard: If you wish to use the mouse, you should move the mouse pointer to the required item and then 'click' the left mouse button. If you wish to use the keyboard, you should hold down the Alt key and then press the keyboard key corresponding to the initial underlined letter.

The choice of keyboard or mouse operation is personal. It is generally considered that the keyboard method is faster as the operator's fingers are usually hovering over the 'QWERTY' section. However, you may prefer to use the mouse at first until you have learned all the keyboard commands. You may also find it quicker to move the insertion pointer when editing by using the mouse. Be aware of both techniques and practise them while you are learning to use the program.

When you have become proficient through regular practice, you may find that you have adopted a combination of mouse and keyboard use, automatically selecting the quickest or most suitable method for the task in hand.

Exercise 2B

Your name

INTRODUCTION TO WORD FOR WINDOWS

When you start using Word for Windows, your screen will show the name of the application in the title bar at the top. Immediately below this you will see the menu bar, containing a horizontal list of words, each with the initial letter underlined.

The majority of functions in Word for Windows can be operated by using either the mouse or the keyboard. Clicking on an icon in the standard tool bar (below the menu bar) is probably easiest at first as the icons are easily remembered. However, there are many short-cut keyboard methods, mainly using the Ctrl key in conjunction with a keyboard character, which can save time.

The choice of keyboard or mouse operation is personal. It is generally considered that the keyboard method is faster as the operator's fingers are usually hovering over the 'QWERTY' section. However, you may prefer to use the mouse at first until you have learned all the keyboard commands. You may also find it quicker to move the insertion pointer when editing by using the mouse. Be aware of both techniques and practise them while you are learning to use the program.

If you wish to use the mouse, you should move the mouse pointer to the required item and then 'click' the left mouse button. If you wish to use the keyboard, you should hold down the Alt key and then press the keyboard key corresponding to the initial underlined letter.

When you have become proficient through regular practice, you may find that you have adopted a combination of mouse and keyboard use, automatically selecting the quickest or most suitable method for the task in hand.

INTRODUCTION TO WORD FOR WINDOWS

Exercise 3C

Your name

INTRODUCTION TO WORD FOR WINDOWS

When you start using Word for Windows, your screen will show the name of the application in the title bar at the top. Immediately below this you will see the menu bar, containing a horizontal list of words, each with the initial letter underlined.

The majority of functions in Word for Windows can be operated by using either the mouse or the keyboard. Clicking on an icon in the standard tool bar (below the menu bar) is probably easiest at first as the icons are easily remembered. However, there are many short-cut keyboard methods, mainly using the Ctrl key in conjunction with a keyboard character, which can save time.

The choice of keyboard or mouse operation is personal. It is generally considered that the keyboard method is faster as the operator's fingers are usually hovering over the 'QWERTY' section. However, you may prefer to use the mouse at first until you have learned all the keyboard commands. You may also find it quicker to move the insertion pointer when editing by using the mouse. Be aware of both techniques and practise them while you are learning to use the program.

If you wish to use the mouse, you should move the mouse pointer to the required item and then 'click' the left mouse button. If you wish to use the keyboard, you should hold down the Alt key and then press the keyboard key corresponding to the

initial underlined letter.

When you have become proficient through regular practice, you may find that you have adopted a combination of mouse and keyboard use, automatically selecting the quickest or most suitable method for the task in hand.

INTRODUCTION TO WORD FOR WINDOWS

Exercise 3B

Your name

INTRODUCTION TO WORD FOR WINDOWS

When you start using Word for Windows, your screen will show the name of the application in the title bar at the top. Immediately below this you will see the menu bar, containing a horizontal list of words, each with the initial letter underlined.

The majority of functions in Word for Windows can be operated by using either the mouse or the keyboard. Clicking on an icon in the standard tool bar (below the menu bar) is probably easiest at first as the icons are easily remembered. However, there are many short-cut keyboard methods, mainly using the Ctrl key in conjunction with a keyboard character, which can save time.

The choice of keyboard or mouse operation is personal. It is generally considered that the keyboard method is faster as the operator's fingers are usually hovering over the 'QWERTY' section. However, you may prefer to use the mouse at first until you have learned all the keyboard commands. You may also find it quicker to move the insertion pointer when editing by using the mouse. Be aware of both techniques and practise them while you are learning to use the program.

If you wish to use the mouse, you should move the mouse pointer to the required item and then 'click' the left mouse button. If you wish to use the keyboard, you should hold down the Alt key and then press the keyboard key corresponding to the initial underlined letter.

When you have become proficient through regular practice, you may find that you have adopted a combination of mouse and keyboard use, automatically selecting the quickest or most suitable method for the task in hand.

INTRODUCTION TO WORD FOR WINDOWS

Exercise 4A

When you start using Word for Windows, your screen will show the name of the application in the title bar at the top. Immediately below this you will see the menu bar, containing a horizontal list of words, each with the initial character underlined.

You can select an item in the menu bar by using the mouse or the keyboard: If you wish to use the mouse, you should move the mouse pointer to the required item and then 'click' the left mouse button. If you wish to use the keyboard, you should hold down the Alt key and then press the keyboard key corresponding to the initial underlined character.

The choice of keyboard or mouse operation is personal. It is generally considered that the keyboard method is faster as the operator's fingers are usually hovering over the 'QWERTY' section. However, you may prefer to use the mouse at first until you have learned all the keyboard commands. You may also find it quicker to move the insertion pointer when editing by using the mouse. Be aware of both techniques and practise them while you are learning to use the program.

When you have become proficient through regular practice, you may find that you have adopted a combination of mouse and keyboard use, automatically selecting the quickest or most suitable method for the task in hand.

Exercise 4B

Your name

INTRODUCTION TO WORD FOR WINDOWS

When you start operating Word for Windows, your screen will show the name of the application in the title bar at the top. Immediately below this you will see the menu bar, containing a horizontal list of words, each with the initial letter underlined.

The majority of functions in Word for Windows can be operated by operating either the mouse or the keyboard. Clicking on an icon in the standard tool bar (below the menu bar) is probably easiest at first as the icons are easily remembered. However, there are many short-cut keyboard methods, mainly operating the Ctrl key in conjunction with a keyboard character, which can save time.

The choice of keyboard or mouse operation is personal. It is generally considered that the keyboard method is faster as the operator's fingers are usually hovering over the 'QWERTY' section. However, you may prefer to use the mouse at first until you have learned all the keyboard commands. You may also find it quicker to move the insertion pointer when editing by operating the mouse. Be aware of both techniques and practise them while you are learning to use the program.

If you wish to use the mouse, you should move the mouse pointer to the required item and then 'click' the left mouse button. If you wish to use the keyboard, you should hold down the Alt key and then press the keyboard key corresponding to the initial underlined letter.

When you have become proficient through regular practice, you may find that you have adopted a combination of mouse and keyboard use, automatically selecting the quickest or most suitable method for the task in hand.

INTRODUCTION TO WORD FOR WINDOWS

Exercise 4C

THE PALACE OF KNOSSOS

It is the largest of the four palaces on the island of Crete to have been excavated. It covers an area of 22,000 square miles and is several storeys high.

The palace was discovered by the English archaeologist, Arthur Evans, who worked with deep scholarly knowledge and enthusiasm to bring to light the most perfect and impressive creation of Minoan architecture.

Extraordinary works of art were uncovered, astonishing the whole world. Statuettes of precious materials, outstanding stone ritual vessels, splendid paintings and other admirable objects were unearthed between 1900-1935.

Exercise 5D

GARDEN WALLS

BRICKS

There are literally *hundreds* of different bricks available but not all of them are suitable for use in the garden.

Common bricks - fairly dull and uninteresting in appearance.

Facing bricks - have an attractive appearance and are usually the ones used for the outsides of homes. A wide variety of **colours** and **textures** is available, some of which weather better than others. Many facing bricks have the special appearance only onto three of the four brick faces which could pose a problem.

Engineering bricks - particularly **dense**, **strong** and **water resistant**. They are sometimes used for brickwork below ground level, damp-proof courses or in a soil-retaining wall.

Exercise 6B

ROCK GARDENS

A rock garden is essentially an informal arrangement of rocks encompassing a collection of alpine and other small plants. The rocks should be set out in a non-uniform manner in order to resemble a natural rock outcrop. There should be little soil showing and an abundance of plant life thriving in conditions reflecting their natural habitat.

The growing medium should be suitable for alpine plants, with just sufficient moisture for their needs in summer and very good drainage and protection from lying damp in winter.

Many alpine plants have long roots which penetrate deep into rock crevices and into moist pockets of soil under and behind rocks.

The cost will largely depend on your choice of alpines, the local availability of suitable stone, access by lorries, and general handling costs.

It is always useful to visit a few rock gardens before planning your own layout. Study them carefully and consider what is entailed. Remember that, once established, the rock garden is a more or less permanent feature - so it makes good sense to put some thought into it and get it right first time.

Exercise 6D

TRAVELLING BY AIR WITH YOUNG CHILDREN

An interminable airport delay is fraught for everyone, but with young children can be quite traumatic. If you are planning to travel abroad by air, expect the worst and go prepared!

Loose-fitting garments (such as cotton tracksuits) in layers that can be peeled on and off as the temperature varies are the most suitable clothing. Trainer type trackshoes, however, can be hot.

Make up a child's pack of time-consuming games, books, puzzles, pens and colouring pencils. Include a special treat such as the child's favourite packet of sweets or a drink. There are a number of travel games available nowadays in the shops which are specially designed for playing 'on the move'. Some of these have special magnetic playing boards to prevent pieces from being lost.

Pass some time in the spectator gallery watching planes land and take off.

Pack enough food and drink in hand luggage to allow for delay on the move.

Don't forget several changes of nappy if you are travelling with a baby. Most UK airports have a mother and baby room to make changing and feeding less of a hassle.

Exercise 8A

WINDOW BOXES AND HANGING BASKETS

The compost should be a compound of sterilized soil and peat, with a proprietary fertilizer. Extra feeding with a granular or liquid fertilizer, preferably organic, will be imperative. Wood and plastic are good construction materials: wire should be galvanized or plastic coated.

Array according to height and habit. Trailing plants such as nasturtiums, geraniums, thunbergia and campanula isophylla should be placed in the foreground or sides. Bushy specimens are best placed centrally - look for alyssum, begonia, impatiens and iberis.

The colours of the blooms should be considered and most people favour a variety of brilliant shades to brighten a dismal wall or a drab street window. Foliage can be utilised to great effect in this respect with variegated leaves being very popular.

Take pains not to overfeed and preclude dehydration by watering two or three times weekly. Renew exhausted soil systematically to ensure success and to minimise the risk of disease and infestation.

Exercise 7A

BREAD IS GOOD FOR YOUR HEALTH

Contrary to popular belief, bread is not a fattening food. Instead, it provides protein, vitamins and minerals necessary for good health and many health experts actually recommend increasing the amount of fibre-rich starchy foods like bread into our diets. It is the fat you spread on bread that makes it fattening.

The type of flour used dictates the colour, flavour and texture of the bread. Most bread in England is made from wheat flour - wholemeal is considered to be a 'health' food as it has nothing added or taken away from the original grain, brown usually contains 85% of the original grain since most of the bran and germ are removed, and white usually contains 75% of the grain.

To keep bread fresher, store it at room temperature in a clean well-ventilated container. Putting bread in the refrigerator makes it stale more quickly. However, bread freezes very well and can be toasted from frozen. Bread cubes and crumbs can be prepared in advance and frozen until required.

There is a wide variety of breads available - white, wholemeal, rye, granary etc. It also comes in a variety of appearances - sliced or unsliced loaves, rolls, muffins, bagels, croissants.

Exercise 8A

SERVICE TO TEACHERS AND LECTURERS

The Education Resource Service offers a wide range of materials covering all aspects of the history and progress of technology in the chemical industry. Our aim is to give students and pupils a better understanding of the way that technology affects their everyday lives.

In addition to a comprehensive range of resource packs, booklets, worksheets, videos and training notes, guidance is given on the National Curriculum. The materials are suited to all ages and are divided by Key Stages.

A new initiative being developed within the Service in conjunction with other agencies, is that of teacher placement. The rapid rate of change means that it is vital that our educators are equipped to deal with projects related to industrial practice and the new placement scheme hopes to assist in this.

Exercise 9B

BOOKING YOUR HOLIDAY

When you read the advertisements in the newspapers, you will feel that you definitely need a holiday. The small advertisements ask you to telephone or to write for more details. You will then receive a brochure for each separate company which is advertising. Flicking through the leaflets with their glossy pictures will encourage you to believe that each destination is the best - the choice is difficult.

Before booking your accommodation, check that the company concerned is a member of an organisation responsible for maintaining standards within the industry. Such an organisation would recommend that only such a business should be used. Take the opportunity to discuss your requirements with an agent and with friends. A good reference from someone else can put your mind at rest.

Exercise 8B

THE POLITICAL AND ADMINISTRATIVE SYSTEM IN FRANCE

France is divided into 22 regions, each comprising up to five 'departements'. These departements are made up of smaller units called 'communes'. Elected representatives are grouped into 'conseils' at each level. A president presides over a regional counseil and a 'maire' leads a commune. These leaders have substantial influence as they are frequently also members of parliament in the 'assemblee nationale' or in the 'senat'.

Companies in France are classified according to the number of employees and not according to their mode of ownership. Companies contracting up to 500 people are known as 'petites et moyennes entreprises'. Few concerns are greater than this, the majority having between 10 and 100 employees. There remains a large number of associations still controlled by founding families and privately owned. However, France also has one of the largest nationalised sectors in Western Europe, ranging from banking and insurance to aluminium, aerospace and chemicals.

The French are extraordinarily legalistic and function within an environment of complex, contradictory and incomprehensible laws. The paradox arises in the French delectation in flouting the law! Seemingly over-bureaucratic procedures are obligatory when conducting business in France and managers are often products of the prestigious business and engineering colleges which exist alongside the universities, and to which entry is arduous.

Exercise 10A

THE HOMOEOPATHIC ALTERNATIVE

At the beginning of the 19th century, a German physician named Samuel Hahnemann introduced more gentle methods of treating the common diseases and ailments of the time.

He used natural substances of plant, animal and mineral origin.

The effectiveness of the remedies was proved through the treatment of malaria with Quinine bark. The approach and attitudes to the patient established in the early days have remained the same. All the factors affecting the patient are considered - both emotional and physical.

A remedy is chosen not only to fit the symptoms but also to suit the individual and his/her lifestyle.

Homoeopathy definitely suits the modern approach to medicine where the patient wants to be involved in and take more responsibility for their own well-being.

Exercise 9C

FRENCH POLISHING

This method of treating wood gives the best finish for furniture. The method was introduced into Europe in the sixteenth century and was developed by a French cabinet maker in the early nineteenth century.

Wood can only be stained to a darker shade. If a lighter shade is required it must be bleached with a wood bleach and then stained. Preparation of the surface is extremely important as flaws become more apparent under French Polish.

Wax and grease can be removed with white spirit and fine steel wool but a very bad finish may need stripping completely.

Exercise 9E

PIZZA PRONTO

In this country, everyone tends to think of Italian food in terms of take-away pizzas and ready-made lasagnes, but traditional cooking in Italy normally demands hours of preparation. Meals rarely consist of one course only.

Although fresh pasta has a much better taste than the dried variety, making the dough, which then needs rolling and cutting, takes hours. The pace of modern life, especially in the northern cities, means that the use of bottled and canned sauces is increasing.

If the basic ingredients of pastas, herbs and sauces are of good quality, then perhaps the results will be acceptable - at least for weekdays.

Exercise 11B

27 Bridge Road
Moorby Park
SELLERSBY
SL3 1RB

today's date

Mr D Tillotson
27 Marsh Lane
SELLERSBY
SL2 4ER

Dear David

May I take this opportunity to thank you once again for the excellent luncheon which my wife and I enjoyed at your home last Sunday.

It was much more relaxing to be able to discuss business in such pleasant surroundings, away from the pressures of the usual office demands.

I feel confident that we will definitely be able to expand on our marketing plans. I shall recommend to the Marketing Team that we commence a re-draft of our standard company advertisement in line with the modifications we discussed.

Please convey my sincere thanks to your wife for her hospitality.

Yours sincerely

George Frazer

Exercise 10B

SHATTERING THE PEACE

Aircraft, traffic, alarms, neighbours - excessive noise is a serious matter. It can cause nuisance and great distress. The effects are difficult to assess because what irritates one person slightly can drive another person to distraction and damage their health. It all depends on the length of time, the amount and the type of noise, as well as on the individual's personality and disposition.

Whilst most people are prepared to tolerate noise which has a recognisable purpose and a limited time span, such as a car alarm or road works, a noise problem which continues for a very long time, disturbing life to a great extent, can cause extreme reactions.

Regulations and bye-laws exist to control the incidence of noise and complaints should be made to the nearest Environmental Health Office.

Complaints usually fall into the following categories:

Noisy neighbours
Building sites and road works
Burglar and car alarms
Pubs, clubs and restaurants
Aircraft and traffic.

Task 12A

13 Benington Avenue
LEEDS
LS3 4PR

today's date

Mrs K Begum
Hotel Attoria
23 Latterley Crescent
SHEFFIELD
SH3 9TR

Dear Mrs Begum

In response to your recent advertisement, I would like to request further information about the special accommodation rates available at your hotel during August.

My wife and I would like to take a long weekend break from Friday-Monday in the second week of August. We shall require a twin-bedded room with adjoining en suite facilities.

I would appreciate it if you could recommend any interesting evening entertainment which is taking place in the area at the time of our stay along with the names of any reputable local restaurants.

I will forward the necessary deposit to secure the booking as soon as I have received the relevant details from you.

Yours sincerely

M Norton (Mr)

Task 12C

Safety on the Road

Car designers now take safety even more seriously. Safety features sell cars. Perhaps in the past, buyers wanted speed, status and glamour but they are now more conscious of safety. Advertisements offer a range of key features:

Side-impact bars
Airbags
Anti-lock brakes
Seatbelt grabbers and tensioners
Rear 3-point seatbelts
Integrated children's seats

EC tests are currently being updated, particularly with reference to side and offset impacts. Car designers are anticipating recommendations and competing for buyers on the safety issue.

The Department of Transport has published a list of the safest cars but models less than 3 years old are not yet included.

Task 12D

SAFETY ON THE ROAD

Car manufacturers now take safety even more seriously. Safety features sell cars. Perhaps in the past, buyers wanted speed, status and glamour but they are now more conscious of safety. Advertisements offer a range of key features:

Side-impact bars
Airbags
Anti-lock brakes
Seatbelt grabbers and tensioners
Rear 3-point seatbelts
Integrated children's seats

EC tests are currently being updated, particularly with reference to side and offset impacts. Car manufacturers are anticipating recommendations and competing for buyers on the safety issue.

    Designers are definitely working to improve the modern car

    and improvements are continually being made but safety is

    now very much a marketing feature and the buyer is left to

    assess which devices are really effective.

The Department of Transport has published a list of the safest cars but models less than 3 years old are not yet included.

SAFETY ON THE ROAD

Task 13A

27 Sunnybank Avenue
HARROGATE
HR5 2SP

today's date

R Melling & Son Ltd
32 Richmond Road
NOTTINGHAM
NG7 8WR

Dear Sirs

I have recently received copies of your catalogue and price list for dried flower arrangements and silk plants.

Unfortunately, I believe the prices quoted may no longer be accurate as the copies were passed to me through a friend some considerable time ago. I would, therefore, appreciate it if you could send me an up-to-date catalogue and price list for which I enclose a large stamped addressed envelope.

There is a reference in your old brochure to ranges of raffia, cane and basketware which you also supply and I would be very interested in receiving more details on these.

I look forward to hearing from you shortly.

Yours faithfully

L De Sousa (Miss)

Exercise 15A

M E M O R A N D U M

FROM: Mariah Fenn, Personnel Manager   **REF:** CZ/386/mf

TO: All Staff   **DATE:** today's

MARKETING SEMINAR

Any members of staff wishing to reserve a place on the 2-day marketing seminar should request an application form and complete this immediately. Forms are available through the company secretary.

In order for the application to be considered, it will be necessary to also obtain the signature of your line manager.

To ensure that sufficient places are available to meet expected demand, it would be helpful if line managers could notify the secretary with details of approximately how many staff in their department they believe will be likely to take advantage of this opportunity.

Unfortunately, the management are unable to guarantee places until they have received full application lists along with any associated expense details.

Please quote Reference **CZ386** at top right of your application form.

Task 13C

COMMUNICATING WITH WORDS

It could be said that the first IT revolution took place over 500 years ago when printing with movable type was invented by Johannes Gutenberg. The armies of scribes and manuscript makers (early word processing operators?) gave way to the production of books by mechanical means although the printing styles imitated handwritten work.

It is ironic that, in the midst of another IT revolution, calligraphy is making a come-back. The practice of calligraphy, which means 'beautiful handwriting' was first revived during the Arts and Crafts movement at the end of last century.

Task 13D

COMMUNICATING WITH WORDS

It could be said that the first information technology revolution took place over 500 years ago when printing with movable type was invented by Johannes Gutenberg. The armies of scribes and manuscript makers (early word processing operators?) gave way to the production of books by mechanical means although the printing styles imitated handwritten work.

    Mass communications are obviously best transmitted by the

    wonders of information technology, but calligraphy allows

    the production of a unique, personalised and creative

    document, and the grace and beauty of the letterforms make

    such an item rather special.

It is ironic that, in the midst of another information technology revolution, calligraphy is making a come-back. The practice of calligraphy, which means 'beautiful handwriting' was first revived during the Arts and Crafts movement at the end of last century.

COMMUNICATING WITH WORDS

Exercise 16A

GARDEN WALLS

BRICKS

There are literally *hundreds* of different bricks available but not all of them are suitable for use in the garden.

<u>Common bricks</u> - fairly dull and uninteresting in appearance.

<u>**Facing bricks**</u> - have an attractive appearance and are usually the ones used for the outsides of homes. A wide variety of **colours** and **textures** is available, some of which weather better than others. many facing bricks have the special appearance only onto three of the four brick faces which could pose a problem.

<u>**Engineering bricks**</u> - particularly **dense, strong** and **water resistant**. they are sometimes used for brickwork below ground level, damp-proof courses or in a soil-retaining wall.

Exercise 16B

MEMORANDUM

FROM: Mariah Fenn, Personnel Manager   REF: Z/386/mf

TO: All Staff   DATE: today's

<u>MARKETING SEMINAR</u>

Any members of staff wishing to reserve a place on the 2-day marketing seminar should request an application form and complete this immediately. Forms are available through the company secretary.

In order for the application to be considered, it will be necessary to also obtain the signature of your line manager.

To ensure that sufficient places are available to meet expected demand, it would be helpful if line managers could notify the secretary with details of approximately how many staff in their department they believe will be likely to take advantage of this opportunity.

Unfortunately, the management are unable to guarantee places until they have received full application lists along with any associated expense.

Please quote Reference **CZ386** at top right of your application form.

Exercise 16D

MAYNESBURY MUSEUMS

There are a number of interesting tourist attractions at Maynesbury:

1) MAYNESBURY HALL: Period house and Local History Museum dating in part from the 15th century with 18th century wing designed by Andrew Browning. Displays of costume and pottery and a 'ghost' room.

2) MAYNESBURY MANOR: Small Tudor Manor House built on the site of a Roman fort with exposed Roman wall in grounds. Displays of Roman archaeological material.

3) BRAMSWELL HOUSE: Noted for its collection of pictures, Chippendale furniture and fine porcelain. There is also a bird garden, a lakeside walk and a children's playground.

Please contact the Maynesbury Information Centre, on 0458 389256, for details of:

    I. Reduced entrance rates for parties of 15 or more.

    II. Special discounts for OAPs and the unwaged.

    III. Opening and closing times.

Exercise 17A

TRAINING PLAN

The aim of our training plan is to give all employees the opportunity to develop themselves so that they can effectively contribute to the achievement of the company's objectives. As a manufacturer of women's fashion accessories, we believe that it is necessary to recruit staff who have received excellent prior training, whether it be as a designer, a secretary or a machine operator.

Although the Personnel Department has been responsible for training in the past, we must now acknowledge that it is necessary to create a separate department for staff training. The new Training Department will be based at the Castle Avenue site and the following members of staff will be transferred to the Department.

An advertisement for the following new appointments is going to press immediately and the persons appointed should be in post by the end of October. Temporary posts may be offered in some cases.

The first task will be to define overall training needs within the framework of the business plan and taking into account existing staff experience.

An analysis of the skills and knowledge required in the performance of every job may take some time but will be a valuable exercise. The analysis should result in a comprehensive and ultimately successful training plan.

Exercise 17B

MOVING INTO MANAGEMENT

Senior management positions in a company are often filled by external applicants as an injection of new blood, but lower down the organisational scale, existing employees are frequently promoted.

There are two main reasons for the latter policy:

using an existing employee's knowledge of the organisation

promotion as a reward or spur.

Performance appraisal can usually provide sufficient evidence of an employee's suitability for further development and the type of management training which would be needed can be easily identified. Management training may be made available in several ways:

Managers need special characteristics, qualities and relevant previous experience if they are to be successful. A degree of flexibility and adaptability is required and they should be aware of the economic, political and social environment. Management training methods can be selected to suit a particular company or a specific situation:

Companies go to considerable expense to pay for training and it is therefore vital that a full evaluation is carried out. A pattern of continuous feedback should be established to review the success of the programmes. Without good management, which responds both to the needs of the company and to the individual skills and attributes of the employees, a business is unlikely to succeed.

Exercises 18A and 18B

Our ref: WP/(your initials)

(today's date)

FOR THE ATTENTION OF LEARNERS

Open Learning Section
Text Production College
Winword Way
READING
RD4 2WP

Dear Sir or Madam

FULLY-BLOCKED BUSINESS LETTER

Following some work study research about 30 years ago, it was decided that business letters could be more quickly prepared if the fully-blocked style were adopted. Every line begins at the left margin - there is no indentation.

At the same time, open punctuation was also introduced. Typists were requested to use commas, full stops etc only in the main body of the letter to make sure that it made sense.

You may be required to include a simple table within your letter. An example is given below:

TOWN OR CITY	COUNTY	COUNTRY
Chesterfield	Derbyshire	England
Coventry	Warwickshire	England
Stranraer	Dumfries and Galloway	Scotland
Swansea	West Glamorgan	Wales

Word Processing examinations have always required a high degree of accuracy.

Elementary examinations usually include a business letter and you should follow the layout you are now learning.

Yours faithfully

W P T Utor

Exercises 18C and 18D

Our ref HOMINS/9987334

(today's date)

PRIVATE

Mrs G H Robins
Sherwood
St John's Crescent
NOTTINGHAM
NG6 8PP

Dear Madam

HOME AND CONTENTS INSURANCE

Further to your recent telephone call to this office, I have pleasure in giving you details of the types of cover we can offer. I enclose a copy of our HOMEPLUS scheme which I hope will be of interest to you.

As I explained to you on the telephone, it is better to insure buildings and contents under one policy so that you can be certain that everything is covered. The policy will cover your house, furniture and personal belongings, including money, valuables and the contents of your freezer.

The claim limits are as follows:

BUILDINGS	CONTENTS	VALUABLES	CASH
Set by valuer	£12,000	£10,000	£500

(The limit for individual items under Contents and Valuables is £1,000)

I hope that this information is sufficient for you. As one of the largest insurers in the United Kingdom, we look after the homes of millions of families. We also offer a full range of insurance and investment services and would be pleased to discuss these with you at any time.

Yours faithfully
NORMAN CASTLE PLC

T Fryer (Ms)

Enc

Exercise 19A

COVERING THE WALLS

Wallpaper first came into being as an inexpensive way of making walls more attractive. Wallpaper may not seem particularly cheap to us nowadays but home decorating is a job which most of us can tackle with practice.

Special effects can be achieved by different types and colours of paper. A lightweight paper is suitable for bedrooms, while a vinyl-coated paper is a practical choice for bathrooms and kitchens as it can be wiped clean.

Estimate the number of rolls you will need carefully <u>before</u> you go shopping. Wallcoverings are made in batches and you can only be certain of an exact colour match if the rolls show the same batch number. It is a good idea to buy slightly more than you require and, provided you have not taken the sellophane wrapping off, some retailers will accept return of unused rolls and give a refund or a credit note.

Time spent on preparation is well spent although not the most exciting part of the process. Old wallpaper can be removed by scraping when wet, by chemical strippers or, if particularly stubborn, by steam stripping. If the walls are not as smooth as they should be or if the wallpaper to be applied is thin, a lining paper may be needed. This is usually applied in the opposite direction to the top paper - horizontally on walls, and parallel with main doors and windows on ceilings.

Take care when using ladders or scaffolding. Make sure they are stable and don't let children play on them. When working around light fittings and switch covers, always switch off electricity at the mains.

Exercise 19C

COVERING THE WALLS

Wallpaper first came into being as an inexpensive way of making walls more attractive. Wallpaper may not seem particularly cheap to us nowadays but home decorating is a job which most of us can tackle with practice.

Special effects can be achieved by different types and colours of paper. A lightweight paper is suitable for bedrooms, while a vinyl-coated paper is a practical choice for bathrooms and kitchens as it can be wiped clean.

Time spent on preparation is well spent although not the most exciting part of the process. Old wallpaper can be removed by scraping when wet, by chemical strippers or, if particularly stubborn, by steam stripping. If the walls are not as smooth as they should be or if the wallpaper to be applied is thin, a lining paper may be needed. This is usually applied in the opposite direction to the top paper - horizontally on walls, and parallel with main doors and windows on ceilings.

Take care when using ladders or scaffolding. Make sure they are stable and don't let children play on them. When working around light fittings and switch covers, always switch off electricity at the mains.

Estimate the number of rolls you will need carefully <u>before</u> you go shopping. Wallcoverings are made in batches and you can only be certain of an exact colour match if the rolls show the same batch number. It is a good idea to buy slightly more than you require and, provided you have not taken the sellophane wrapping off, some retailers will accept return of unused rolls and give a refund or a credit note.

Exercise 19D

THE YORKSHIRE AND HUMBERSIDE REGION

This famous region of England covers a large area stretching from Spurn Point on the East coast to the picturesque village of Clapham in the Pennines. Its northern boundary stretches to Teesside while the southern border, south of Sheffield, borders Derbyshire.

The attractions of Humberside include approximately 80 kilometres of safe, sandy beaches. Maritime heritage centres and traditional seaside towns prevail on the coast while inland are attractive market towns and historic halls. The longest single span suspension bridge in the world - the Humber Bridge - is definitely a sight worth seeing.

The landscape of North Yorkshire is more dramatic with large expanses of wild moors, steep-sided valleys and a host of medieval castles and abbeys. The coastline is striking with its high cliffs and sweeping bays, providing lovely settings for the resorts of Scarborough and Whitby.

Industrial museums exist also in West Yorkshire, with emphasis on the textile industry. The cities of Leeds, Bradford and Halifax demonstrate the prosperity of the area in the 19th century through the magnificent municipal buildings. There are lots of other museums to interest the visitor, ranging from the Bronte Parsonage at Haworth to the National Museum of Photography, Film and Television in Bradford.

South Yorkshire was said to be the crucible of the industrial revolution - the heart of the coal and steel industries. Industrial heritage is a particular feature of the cities and towns yet a short drive will bring you to spectacular, open countryside.

North Yorkshire is the largest of the four areas within the region with Humberside as second largest. The areas of West Yorkshire and South Yorkshire, although smaller in terms of square miles, are much more densely populated.

Task 20B

M E M O R A N D U M

FROM: Val Feathers, Headmistress   REF: FR/VF

TO: All Staff   DATE: today's

SCHOOL FUND-RAISING FOR MATERIALS

Please make a note in your diary of the following fund-raising events which are scheduled to help the school to raise additional money for badly-needed materials.

I would be grateful if you could support the events wherever possible and offers of assistance are definitely welcome.

A) Jumble Sale. The jumble sale will be held in the school hall, Thursday 27 October at 7.30 pm. Please bring all your unwanted jumble, bric-a-brac and miscellaneous items to the school office at least 2 days before the sale. Volunteers to man the sale are needed urgently.

B) Clothes Party. Mrs Versity has kindly volunteered the use of her home for a 'chainstore seconds clothes party'. You can call in at any time during the afternoon of Saturday, 29 October and try on any of the clothes on display - I am told these will be on sale at vastly reduced prices from those in the normal high street shops and catalogues. Mrs Versity will donate the 10% commission on all goods sold towards the purchase of new school materials.

C) Trivia Quiz Night. Following the last successful 'Trivia Quiz Night', we shall now hold a second event. The evening will be held at The Wayfarers Inn. We urgently need four teams. Please contact Mr Halstead if it's at all possible for you to be a team player.

If you have any other suggestions for fund-raising events, please let me have details as soon as possible. We are in desperate need of two new computers, in addition to other materials needed for the new library.

Task 20A

today's date

URGENT

Mrs K Begum
Hotel Attoria
23 Latterley Crescent
SHEFFIELD
SH3 9TR

Dear Mrs Begum

In response to your recent advertisement, I would like to request further information about the special accommodation rates available at your hotel during August.

My company is interested in booking approximately 4 separate business conferences during August for which we would require sufficient overnight accommodation for delegates attending the conference as well as hiring the conference suite itself.

Details of our requirements are as follows:

CONFERENCE DATE	DELEGATES	SPECIAL REQUIREMENTS
August 2 - August 4	12	3 Vegetarian
August 7 - August 10	10	1 Wheelchair access
August 13 - August 15	8	None
August 26 - August 28	16	4 Vegetarian

I would appreciate it if you could recommend any interesting evening entertainment which is taking place in the area at the time of our stay along with the names of any reputable local restaurants.

I will forward the necessary deposit to secure the booking as soon as I have received the relevant details from you.

Yours sincerely
MERIDIAN MARKETING SERVICES

M Norton (Mr)

Task 20C

MEMORANDUM

FROM: **Val Feathers, Headmistress** REF: **FR/VF**

TO: **All Staff** DATE: **today's**

SCHOOL FUND-RAISING FOR RESOURCES

Please make a note of the following fund-raising events which are scheduled to help the school to raise additional money for badly-needed resources. I would be grateful if you could support the events wherever possible and offers of assistance are especially welcome.

A) **Jumble Sale**. The jumble sale will be held in the School Hall, Thursday 27 October at 7.30 pm. Please bring all your unwanted jumble, bric-a-brac and miscellaneous items to the School Office at least 2 days before the sale. Volunteers to man the sale are needed urgently.

B) **Trivia Quiz Night**. Following the last successful 'Trivia Quiz Night', we shall now hold a second event on Friday, 28 October at 8.30 pm. The evening will be held at The Wayfarers Inn who have kindly agreed to let us have a function room free of charge. We urgently need four teams. Please contact Mr Halstead if it's at all possible for you to be a team player.

C) **Clothes Party**. Mrs Versity has kindly volunteered the use of her home for a 'chainstore seconds clothes party'. You can call in at any time during the afternoon of Saturday, 29 October and try on any of the clothes on display. Mrs Versity will donate the 10% commission on all goods sold towards the purchase of new school resources.

D) **Prize Draw**. Tickets will be available shortly for the prize draw - more details to follow soon.

If you have any other suggestions for fund-raising events, please let me have details as soon as possible. We are in desperate need of two new computers, in addition to other resources needed for the new library.

Task 21A

today's date

For the attention of the Sales Manager

R Melling & Son Ltd
32 Richmond Road
NOTTINGHAM
NG7 8WR

Dear Sirs

I have recently received copies of your catalogue and price list for dried flower arrangements and silk plants.

Unfortunately, I believe the prices quoted may no longer be accurate as the copies were passed to me through a friend some considerable time ago. I would, therefore, appreciate it if you could send me an up-to-date catalogue and price list for which I enclose a large stamped addressed envelope.

My company has recently completely modernised its office layout and we would like to further enhance the decor with floral arrangements. We would be particularly interested to know if you operate a 'hire' service whereby the displays and/or plants can be changed on a regular basis, perhaps monthly. I think it might be useful for you to discuss our exact requirements with the different departmental managers concerned - they can be contacted on the following telephone extension numbers:

DEPARTMENT	MANAGER	EXTENSION
Reception	Susan Evans	2172
Sales	Robert Davies	2110
Marketing	Roman Piatkowski	2134
Secretarial/Administration	Janet Robertshaw	2135

There is a reference in your old brochure to ranges of raffia, cane and basketware which you also supply and I would be very interested in receiving more details on these.

I look forward to hearing from you shortly.

Yours faithfully
FENWAYS & SMITH LTD

L De Sousa (Miss)

Task 21B

THE COMPACT DISK REVOLUTION

The development of the 5" silver saucer with its tremendous storage capability has opened up a whole new world of multimedia products - business applications, educational programs, games and electronic reference books with sound and video.

Audio CDs first appeared when they began to replace vinyl records and cassettes in the 1980s. Manufacturers soon realised the greater potential of this new storage medium and looked towards producing full-screen live video action with CDs replacing videotape.

Full motion video (FMV) is now available at a quality that's claimed to be better than VHS, offering an entire feature film on a couple of disks, lots of music videos on just one, and TV-style video action in computer games.

a) CD-ROM - compact disk read only memory. A disk of 650Mb can store the equivalent data of a thousand floppy disks.

b) CD-i - compact disk interactive. These work similarly to CD-ROM disks, but being produced to a different standard you can't read a CD-i disk on a PC - you need CD-i hardware.

c) CD-R - recordable compact disk drives. Although these are available, the hardware to enable you to record onto a CD is extremely expensive.

A number of telecom companies are planning 'video on demand' services. This is where you simply ring up and request a film or TV programme you want to watch to be transmitted straight down the line to your own individual set.

Task 21C

THE COMPACT DISC REVOLUTION

The development of the 5" silver saucer with its tremendous storage capacity has opened up a whole new world of multimedia products - business applications, educational programs, games and electronic reference books with sound and video.

Manufacturers soon realised the greater potential of this new storage medium and looked towards producing full-screen live video action with CDs replacing videotape.

a) **CD-ROM - compact disc read only memory.** A disc of 650Mb can store the equivalent data of a thousand floppy discs.

b) **CD-i - compact disc interactive.** These work in a similar way to CD-ROM discs, but being produced to a different standard you can't read a CD-i disc on a PC - you need CD-i hardware.

c) **CD-R - recordable compact disc drives.** Although these are available, the hardware to enable you to record onto a CD is extremely expensive. One of the main problems is that you can only write to a CD once - it can't be 'taped over' so you can't re-use the disc space.

Full motion video (FMV) is now available at a quality that's claimed to be better than VHS, offering an entire feature film on a couple of discs, lots of music videos on just one, and TV-style video action in computer games.

A number of telecom companies are now planning 'video on demand' services. This is where you simply ring up and request a film or TV programme to be transmitted straight down the line to your own individual set.

For technical and financial reasons, it seems that videotape will still be around in the 21st century as a convenient, practical and economical way of watching TV programmes and films as, unlike the video demand services being planned by cable and telephone companies, it doesn't incur any additional fees.

Task 21D

MEMORANDUM

FROM:	Sandra Jennings	REF:	SJ/87
TO:	Lewis Waterhouse	DATE:	today's

SNIPPET FOR STAFF EDITORIAL

Here is the small snippet you asked me to write for the staff editorial:

PERFECT PANSIES

Pansies have such a long flowering period and come in so many different colours that they can bring variety to the garden. The ideal site is somewhere where they can have their roots in cool, moist soil and their tops in the sun.

On the other hand, they'd be quite happy to nestle in the dappled shade of larger shrubs.

The compact shape of violas makes them particularly good for edging borders and paths. Both violas and pansies can be grown in containers although it's a pity to restrict the violas' spreading potential.

Progress review checklist

Unit	Topic	Date completed	Comments
1	Load Word for Windows program		
	Open a new document/file		
	Key in text		
	Move cursor around document		
	Edit text (delete/insert)		
	Split/join paragraphs		
	Save work to correct disk drive		
	Print a document		
	Close a file		
	Exit Word for Windows program		
2	Open an existing file		
	Select a block of text		
	Delete/cut a block of text		
	Restore deleted text		
	Move a block of text		
	Copy a block of text		
3	Ragged right margin		
	Justified right margin		
	Units of measurement		
	Change margins		
	Line spacing – double and single		
	Print preview document before printing		
4	Search/find and replace text		
	Spellcheck a document		
5	Bold text		
	Underline text		
	Centre text		
	Change font style		
	Change font size		
6	Consolidation 1		
7	Examination practice 1 (CLAIT)		
8	Unfamiliar/foreign words		
9	Typescript containing:		
	correction signs		
	abbreviations		
	typographical errors		
	errors of agreement		
	Grammar tool		
10	Keying in from manuscript copy		
	Additional correction signs		
11	Personal business letters		
	Insert a new page marker		
	Envelopes		
12	Consolidation 2		
13	Examination practice 2 (core text)		
14	Tabulation		
15	Memorandum		
	Abbreviations		
16	Indent function		
	Change line length of document		
	Enumerated/bulleted items		
17	Allocate vertical space		
	Confirm facts		
18	Business letters		
	Special marks		
	Enclosure marks		
	Automatic date insertion		
19	Rearrange text		
20	Consolidation 3		
21	Examination practice 3 (Level 1)		

Glossary

Action	Keyboard	Mouse	Menu
Allocate clear lines	Press: ↵ once for each line required, plus one		
Allocate vertical space			Format, Paragraphs Key in measurement
Blocked capitals	Press: **Caps lock** key		
Bold text	Press: **Ctrl + B**	Click: **B** on Formatting Tool Bar	Format, Font
Bulleted lists		Click: on Formatting Tool Bar	Format, Bullets and Numbering
Case of letters	Press: **Shift + F3** To capitalize letters: Press: **Ctrl + Shift + A**		Format, Change case
Centre text	Press: **Ctrl + E**	Click: on Formatting Tool Bar	Format, Paragraphs, Indents and Spacing, Alignment
Close a file (clear screen)	Press: **Ctrl + C**		File, Close
Copy a block of text Highlight text to be copied	Press: **Ctrl + C**	Click: on Standard Tool Bar *or* Press: Right mouse button and Select: **Copy**	Edit, Copy
Position cursor where text is to be copied to	Press: **Ctrl + V**	Click: on Standard Tool Bar *or* Press: Right mouse button and select: **Paste**	Edit, Paste
Cursor movement Move cursor to required position	Use arrow keys ↑ ↓ ← →	Click: Left mouse button in required position	
Move to top of document	**Ctrl + Home**		
Move to end of document	**Ctrl + End**		
Move left word by word	**Ctrl + ←**		
Move right word by word	**Ctrl + →**		
Move to end of line	**End**		
Move to start of line	**Home**		
Cut text	*See* Delete/cut a block of text.		
Date insertion	Press: **Alt + Shift + D**		Insert, Date and Time
Delete a character	Move cursor to incorrect character: Press: **Del** *or* Move cursor to right of incorrect character: Press: **←** (Del)		
Delete a word	Move cursor to end of word: Press: **Ctrl + ←** (Del) *or* **Ctrl + X**	Double-click on word to select: Press: Right mouse button Select: **Cut**	Select: Edit, Cut
Delete/cut a block of text	Select incorrect text: Press: **←** (Del) *or* select word: Press: **Ctrl + X**	Select incorrect text: Press: Right mouse button Select: **Cut**	Select incorrect text: Select: Edit, Cut
Exit the program	Press: **Alt + F4**	Double-click control button at left of title bar	File, Exit
Find text	Press: **Ctrl + F**		Edit, Find
Font size	Press: **Ctrl + Shift + P** Choose desired size	Click: **10** on Formatting Tool Bar Choose desired size	Format, Font Choose desired size
Next larger point size	Press: **Ctrl +]**		
Next smaller point size	Press: **Ctrl + [**		
Font typeface style	Press: **Ctrl + Shift + F** Choose desired font	Click: **Times New Roman** on Formatting Tool Bar Choose desired font	Format, Font Choose desired font
Go to (a specified page)	Press: **Ctrl + G** *or* **F5**		Edit, Go To ...
Grammar tool			Tools, Grammar
Help function	Press: **F1** (for contents) Press: **Shift + F1** (for context sensitive help)	Click: on Formatting Tool Bar	Help

Action ☞	*Keyboard*	*Mouse*	*Menu*
Indent function Indent at left to next tab stop	Press: **Ctrl + M**	Click: 📄 on Formatting Tool Bar	**F**ormat, **P**aragraphs, **I**ndents and Spacing
Indent at left to previous tab stop	Press: **Ctrl + Shift + M**		
Indent as a hanging paragraph	Press: **Ctrl + T**		
Unindent and return to standard margins	Press: **Ctrl + Q**	Click: 📄 on Formatting Tool Bar *using ruler:* First-line indent Left indent First-line and left indents Right indent	
Insert a line break	Press: **Shift + ↵**		
Insert a page break	Press: **Ctrl + ↵**		**I**nsert, **B**reak, Page break
Insert special characters/symbols	Press: **Ctrl + Shift + Q**		Position cursor where you want the character/symbol to appear: Select: **I**nsert, **S**ymbol
Insert text	Simply key in the missing character(s) at the appropriate place – the existing text will 'move over' to make room for the new text.		
Italics	Press: **Ctrl + I**	Click: *I* on Formatting Tool Bar	**F**ormat, **F**ont
Justified right margin	Press: **Ctrl + J**	Click: ▤ on Formatting Tool Bar	**F**ormat, **P**aragraphs, **I**ndents and Spacing, Alignment
Line length – to change	Select text. Display horizontal ruler. Move margin markers to required position on ruler.		
Line spacing – to set	Press: **Ctrl + 1** (single) Press: **Ctrl + 2** (double) Press: **Ctrl + 0** (to add or delete a line space)		**F**ormat, **P**aragraphs, **I**ndents and Spacing
Margins (to change)			**F**ile, Page Set**u**p, **M**argins
Move a block of text Select text to be moved Position cursor where text is to be moved to	Press: **Ctrl + X** *or* **F2** Press: **Ctrl + V** *or* **↵** *or* Hold down **Ctrl** and Click: Right mouse button	Click: ✂ on Standard Tool Bar Click: 📋 on Standard Tool Bar *Drag and drop moving:* Select text to be moved Click left mouse button in middle of text and keep held down Drag selection to required location Release mouse button	**E**dit, Cu**t** **E**dit, **P**aste
Move around text quickly Left/right word by word End/start of line Top/bottom of paragraph Up/down one screen Top/bottom of document	Press: **Ctrl + ←** *or* **Ctrl + →** Press: **End** *or* **Home** Press: **Ctrl + ↑** *or* **Ctrl + ↓** Press: **PgUp** *or* **PgDn** Press: **Ctrl + Home** *or* **Ctrl + End**		
Open an existing file	Press: **Ctrl + O**	Click: 📂 on Standard Tool Bar	**F**ile, **O**pen
Open a new file	Press: **Ctrl + N**	Click: 📄 on Standard Tool Bar	**F**ile, **N**ew
Page Setup			**F**ile, Page Set**u**p (Choose from **Margins**, **Paper Size**, **Paper Source** and **Layout**)
Paragraphs – splitting/joining	Make a new paragraph (i.e. split a paragraph into two) Join two consecutive paragraphs into one	Move cursor to first letter of new paragraph Press: **↵** twice Move cursor to first character of second paragraph Press: **←** (**Del**) twice (backspace delete key) Press: **Spacebar** (to insert a space after full stop)	
Print out hard copy	Press: **Ctrl + P**	Click: 🖨 on Standard Tool Bar	**F**ile, **P**rint
Ragged right margin	Press: **Ctrl + L**	Click: ▤ on Formatting Tool Bar	**F**ormat, **P**aragraphs, **I**ndents and Spacing, Alignment
Remove text emphasis	Press: **Ctrl + Spacebar** *or* Press: **Ctrl + Shift + Z**	Select text to be changed back to normal text: Click: Appropriate button on Formatting Tool Bar	**F**ormat, **P**aragraphs, **I**ndents and Spacing
Repeating actions	Press: **F4** to repeat previous action *or* Press: **Ctrl + Y**	Click: ↻ on Formatting Tool Bar	To repeat sets of actions, drag down the **Redo** drop-down list and select the group of actions you wish to repeat

Action	Keyboard	Mouse	Menu

Replace text – typeover	1 Select the incorrect text and then type in the correct entry – Word will fit the replacement text exactly into the original space
	2 Move cursor to incorrect entry:
	  Press: The **Ins** key (typeover on) and overtype with correct entry
	  Press: The **Ins** key again (typeover off) to stop overtyping text		

Restore deleted text	Press: **Ctrl + Z**	Click: 🔲 on Formatting Tool Bar	<u>E</u>dit, <u>U</u>ndo
Ruler – to display			<u>V</u>iew, <u>R</u>uler
Save work to disk Save a file for the first time	Press: **F12**		<u>F</u>ile, Save <u>A</u>s Enter <u>F</u>ilename Select correct <u>D</u>irectory and **Drive** Click on **OK**
Save an active file which has been saved previously	Press: **Ctrl + S** *or* Press: **Shift + F12**	Click: 🔲 on Standard Tool Bar	<u>F</u>ile, <u>S</u>ave
Save *all* open files			<u>F</u>ile, Save All
Scroll bars (to view)			<u>T</u>ools, <u>O</u>ptions, View Select: Hori<u>z</u>ontal scroll bar and <u>V</u>ertical scroll bar options
Search for text	*See* Find text.		
Select text One character (or more) One word	Press: **Shift + ← or →** Press: **Shift + Ctrl + ←** *or →*	Click and drag pointer across text Double-click on word	
To end of line Start of line A full line A paragraph Whole document Any block of text	Press: **Shift + End** Press: **Shift + Home** Press: **Shift + End** *or* **Home** — Press: **Ctrl + A** —	Click and drag pointer right or down Click and drag pointer left or up Click in selection border Double-click in selection border Triple-click in selection border Position pointer at start of text and Press: **Shift**. Then, position pointer at end of text and click	
Remove selection		Click in any white space	
Spaced capitals	Press: **Caps lock** key. Leave one space after each letter. Leave three spaces after each word.		
Spellcheck	Press: **F7**	Click: 🔲 on Standard Tool Bar	<u>T</u>ools, <u>S</u>pelling
Status bar			<u>T</u>ools, <u>O</u>ptions, View Select: Status <u>B</u>ar option
Switch on and load Word		Double-click **Microsoft Word** icon	
Symbols	*See* Insert special characters/symbols.		
Tabulation	Select the paragraph(s) in which you wish to make changes to the tab settings, then either: 1 Select <u>T</u>abs from the F<u>o</u>rmat menu 2 Click the tab marker on the horizontal ruler line to select the type of tab you want, then drag the tab to the required position on the horizontal ruler line (*note:* Drag a tab marker *off* the horizontal ruler line to remove it)		
Text, replace	Press: **Ctrl + H**		<u>E</u>dit, <u>R</u>eplace
Underline text Single word Double word	Press: **Ctrl + U** Press: **Ctrl + Shift + W** Press: **Ctrl + Shift + H**	Click: 🔲 on Formatting Tool Bar	F<u>o</u>rmat, <u>F</u>ont
Undoing actions	Press: **Ctrl + Z**	Click: 🔲 on Standard Tool Bar	To undo sets of actions, drag down the **Undo** drop-down list and select the group of actions you wish to undo
Units of measurement			<u>T</u>ools, <u>O</u>ptions, General <u>M</u>easurement Units Select desired units
View magnified pages		Click: 100% 🔲 on Standard Tool Bar Click: **Magnifies** on print preview	<u>V</u>iew, <u>Z</u>oom
View – normal view	Press: **Ctrl + F2**	Click: 🔲 **Normal** button at bottom left of document window	<u>V</u>iew, <u>N</u>ormal
View – outline view		Click: 🔲 **Outline** button at bottom left of document window	<u>V</u>iew, <u>O</u>utline
View – page layout view		Click: 🔲 **Page Layout** button at bottom left of document window	<u>V</u>iew, <u>P</u>age Layout
View – print preview	Press: **Ctrl + F2**	Click: 🔲 on Standard Tool Bar	<u>F</u>ile, Print Pre<u>v</u>iew